The High 5 Habit

Also by Mel Robbins

Books

The 5 Second Rule: Transform Your Life, Work, and Confidence with Everyday Courage

Audiobook Originals

Take Control of Your Life: How to Silence Fear and Win the Mental Game

Work It Out: The New Rules for Women to Get Ahead at Work

Kick Ass with Mel Robbins

Start Here: Pep Talks for Life

The High 5 Habit

Take control of your life with one simple habit

Mel Robbins

HAY HOUSE, INC.
Carlsbad, California · New York City
London · Sydney · New Delhi

Published in the United States by: Hay House, Inc.: www.hayhouse.com®
Published in Australia by: Hay House Australia Pty. Ltd.: www.hayhouse
.com.au · **Published in the United Kingdom by:** Hay House UK, Ltd.: www
.hayhouse.co.uk · **Published in India by:** Hay House Publishers India: www
.hayhouse.co.in

Project editor: Melody Guy
Cover design: Skye High Interactive, Inc.
Interior design: Skye High Interactive, Inc. and Nick C. Welch
Interior photos/illustrations: Courtesy of the author

Cataloging-in-Publication Data is on file at the Library of Congress

Hardcover ISBN: 978-1-4019-6212-8
E-book ISBN: 978-1-4019-6213-5

10 9 8 7 6 5 4 3 2 1
1st edition, September 2021

Printed in the United States of America

For Chris, Sawyer, Kendall, and Oakley

Contents

CHAPTER 1

You Deserve a High 5 Life

Let me tell you about a day, not very long ago, when I made a simple discovery. I call it the High 5 Habit and it will help you improve the most important relationship in your life—the one you have with yourself. I'm going to share with you the story, the research, and how you can use this habit to change your life too.

It all started one morning as I was standing in my bathroom brushing my teeth, and I caught my reflection in the mirror, and thought:

Ugh.

I started picking apart all the things I don't like about myself—the dark circles under my eyes, my pointy chin, the fact that my right boob is smaller than the left one, and the saggy skin on my stomach. My mind started going: *I look horrible. I need to exercise more. I hate my neck.* Every thought I had just made me feel worse about myself.

I looked at the time—my first Zoom call started in 15 minutes. *I've got to get up earlier.* I thought about the deadline I was up against. The deal I was trying to close. The emails and texts I hadn't responded to. The dog that had yet to be walked. My dad's biopsy results. And all the things the kids needed me to do today. I felt completely overwhelmed and I hadn't even put on a bra or had coffee yet.

Ugh.

All I wanted to do that morning was pour myself a cup of coffee, collapse in front of the TV, and just forget about all the things that were bothering me . . . but I knew that was the wrong thing to do. I knew that no one was going to swoop in and fix my problems or finish the projects on my list or exercise for me or handle that difficult conversation I needed to have at work.

I just wanted . . . a fricking break . . . from my life.

It had been a hell of a few months. The stress was nonstop. I'd been so busy taking care of and worrying about everyone and everything else, who was taking care of me? I'm sure you can relate to that on some level too. In moments like this, when the demands of life pile up and your attitude tanks, it can create a downward spiral.

I needed someone to tell me, *You're right, this is hard. You don't deserve this. It's not fair . . . and if anyone can handle it, it's YOU.* That's what I wanted to hear. I needed reassurance and a pep talk. And, even though I'm one of the most successful motivational speakers in the world, I couldn't think of a single thing to say.

I don't know what came over me. Or why I did it. But for whatever reason, standing there in my bathroom, in my underwear, I lifted my hand to my tired reflection in a kind of salute. *I see you*, was all I wanted to say. *I see you and I love you. Come on now, Mel. You've got this.*

I realized midway through this gesture that my salute to myself was a simple high five. Recognizable, unmistakable, and as common as a handshake. We've all given and received high fives countless times in our lives. Maybe there's even something a little cheesy about them. But there I stood, braless and uncaffeinated, leaning against the bathroom sink, high fiving my own reflection.

Without saying a word, I was telling myself something I desperately needed to hear. I was assuring myself that I could do it, whatever *it* was. I was cheering for myself, and encouraging the woman I saw in the mirror to lift her chin and keep going. As my hand touched the mirror and met my reflection, I felt my spirit lift a little. *I wasn't alone. I had ME.* It was a simple gesture, an act of kindness toward myself. Something I needed, and deserved.

Immediately, I felt my chest loosen, I squared my shoulders, and I cracked a smile at how corny the high five seemed, but suddenly, I didn't look so tired, I didn't feel so alone, and that to-do list didn't seem so daunting. I went on with my day.

The next morning, the alarm went off. Same problems and same overwhelm. I got up. I made my bed. I walked into the bathroom and there was my reflection: *Hey there, Mel.* Without thinking, I smiled and found myself high fiving myself in the mirror again.

On the third morning, I got up and realized I was thinking about and *looking forward* to now seeing my reflection so I could give myself that high five. I know it's weird, but it's the truth. I made my bed a little quicker than usual and walked into the bathroom with a sense of enthusiasm that no one should have at 6:05 A.M. The only way I can describe it:

It felt like I was about to see a friend.

Later that day, I wondered about the times in life when I've gotten a high five. Naturally, I thought about playing team sports when I was younger. I thought about the road races I used to run with my girlfriends. Or watching baseball games at Fenway Park and how the stadium erupts with high fives when the Red Sox score. Or high fiving a friend when they got that promotion, or broke up with that loser, or played the winning hand in a game of cards.

And then I remembered one of the highlights of my life: running the New York City marathon in 2001, just two months after the 9/11 terrorist attacks killed 2,977 people and destroyed the Twin Towers.

For 26.2 miles, spectators jammed the sidewalks and for as far as the eye could see American flags hung from apartment windows in every building as the course wove its way through all five boroughs that make up New York City.

If it had not been for the people watching, who, for 26.2 miles, packed both sides of the route and high fived me and cheered for me, there is no way I would have made it. On my own, I just don't have that kind of Navy SEAL stamina. I get winded carrying groceries up two flights of stairs. At the time, I was a new mom, working full time with two kids under the age of three, who hadn't done the proper training for a race that long. Heck, my sneakers were barely broken in, but it had always been on my bucket list to complete this race, so when I got a chance to run it, I was determined to do it. There were so many moments when my knees buckled, my bladder leaked, and my mind pleaded, *No way. I can't do this.* At times, I slowed to a hobble. *Why didn't I train harder? Why did I buy new sneakers two weeks ago?* Near mile 13, I was begging the volunteers at the water station to agree with me that I should quit. They wouldn't hear it. *Quit? Now? But you've come this far!* Their encouragement silenced my doubt, so off I went.

You are so much stronger than you think.

The only reason I completed that marathon was because of the constant encouragement and celebration I received along the way. If I had listened to the voices in my head, I would have stopped running at about mile seven, when the blisters on my feet tore open and each step became crazy painful. It felt so good to be cheered for— that's what kept my mind focused and my body moving. Those high fives were what fueled my belief that I could in fact do something I had never done before.

When I felt discouraged as so many other runners kept striding past me, it was the slap of a stranger's hand that kept me from quitting. And that's the thing: a high five is so much more than a slap of a hand. It's a transfer of energy and belief from one person to another. It awakens something within you. It's a reminder of something you've forgotten. Every high five said *I believe in you*, which made me believe in myself and in my ability to push forward, step by step, for six hours until I crossed that finish line and achieved that goal.

When you think about the remarkable power of a stranger's high five, it's easy to draw parallels between life and running a marathon. Both are long, rewarding, challenging, and painful at times. Imagine if you woke up every morning and you could tap into that same high five energy cheering you on as you ran through your day-to-day life?

Stop and think about it. How does criticizing yourself actually help you?

What if you could flip that and learn how to cheer yourself forward every day, every week, every year of your life, step by step, as you move toward your goals and your dreams? Just imagine if YOU were your biggest cheerleader, fan, and encourager. It's hard to imagine, isn't it? It shouldn't be.

I want you to answer this question honestly: *How frequently do you cheer for yourself?*

I bet you just came to the same conclusion I did. Almost never.

The question is, *Why?* If being loved, encouraged, and celebrated feels so darn good, if it keeps you going and helps you achieve your goals, why don't you do it for yourself?

It's the old "Put the oxygen mask on yourself first" thing.

I've heard that saying a million times, but the truth is, I never really knew how to do it in my day-to-day life. Boy, did this high five in the mirror open my eyes: to put yourself first, you need to cheer yourself into that position because that's exactly how you put everyone else there.

Think about how great you are at supporting and celebrating other people. Cheering for your favorite teams, following your favorite actors, musicians, and influencers. You buy tickets to their games, give standing ovations at their shows, follow their recommendations, purchase their new clothing lines, and carefully keep track of all their achievements, from Super Bowl wins to Grammy Awards.

You also do a great job of supporting and uplifting the people you love in your own life—your partner, children, best friends, family members, and co-workers. You plan birthday parties and celebrations for everyone in your family, you take on extra work to support your overwhelmed colleague, and you're the first one to pump up your friend when they show you their dating profile (*You look amazing!*) or start a side hustle selling supplements (*I'll take a year's supply*). You encourage everyone else to chase their goals and dreams, including the woman you just met this morning in the yoga class. When the instructor mentioned the upcoming teacher training certification program, you didn't skip a beat: *Are you going to sign up? You should! You have a beautiful downward dog.*

But when it comes to celebrating and encouraging yourself, you not only fall seriously short—you do the opposite. You trash yourself. You look at yourself in the mirror and pick yourself apart. You tear yourself down and argue against your own goals and dreams. You bend over backward for other people and never for yourself.

It's time to give yourself the encouragement you deserve and you need.

Self-worth, self-esteem, self-love, and self-confidence all begin by building those attributes within your SELF. That's why I want you to begin every day with a high five in the mirror. It's a habit you should learn, you should understand, and you should practice every single day. And that's just the beginning.

In this book, you'll learn dozens of ways to make supporting and celebrating yourself a habit. Using research, science, deeply personal stories, and the real-life results that the High 5 Habit is creating in people's lives around the world (and you'll meet a lot of them throughout this book), I'm going to prove to you and inspire you to take control of your life by high fiving yourself in all kinds of cool ways—every single day. The High 5 Habit is more than something you do—it's a holistic approach to life, a proven mind-set, and powerful tools that reprogram the subconscious patterns in your mind.

You will also learn how to identify the thoughts and beliefs that take you down mentally, like guilt, jealousy, fear, anxiety, and insecurity. And more importantly, you will practice flipping them into new thought and behavior patterns that lift you up and keep you moving forward. And of course, I'm going to break all this down and show you how to do it, explain the research that proves why these tools work, and I'll even be there supporting you every day (more to come on that soon).

This is bigger than knowing how to wake up happy, or pick yourself up when you're feeling down, or hype yourself up for the biggest and most exciting moments of your life (all of which you'll learn how to do in this book).

It is about understanding and improving the most important relationship you have in the world—the one with your SELF. In these pages, you'll learn about your most fundamental needs and how to fill them. You'll also discover proven mindset strategies to help you get through *every* moment—the highs and lows, ups and downs— and never give up on the person you're staring at in the mirror.

How you see yourself is how you see the world.

As you might imagine, I've thought a lot about high fives in the process of writing this book, probably more than anyone should. What I realize now, after practicing the High 5 Habit, is that I've spent the first half of my life picking apart my reflection or alto-gether ignoring the woman I saw reflected back. It's ironic when you consider what I do for a living.

As one of the most booked motivational speakers and best-selling authors in the world, my job is to give you the tools and the encouragement you need to change your life. My confidence in you gives YOU confidence in you. When I really stop and think about it, my job is the embodiment of a high five. Everything I share— whether it's on the stage, or in books, YouTube videos, online courses, and social media posts—every single thing I do is meant to tell you *I believe in you. Your dreams matter. You've got this, keep going.*

I've been giving you high fives for years.

And even though I've been high fiving you, I haven't always been that great at giving them to myself. I am my own worst critic. I bet you are yours. It's only recently, when I started high fiving myself, first in the mirror and then in so many other symbolic ways, that things fell into place. When you learn how to see and support yourself, it gets easier to catch those moments when you start going mentally low and flip into a more powerful and opti-mistic frame of mind. With a positive mind, you'll be motivated to take positive actions to change your life. When you're equipped with that kind of high five energy and attitude, you can make anything happen.

When I stopped trashing myself and started giving my reflection a high five instead, it was more than an encouraging gesture on a low day. It flipped that self-criticism and self-hatred on its head. It changed the lens through which I viewed my life. That was the beginning of a massive shift in my life. A line in the sand. The beginning of a brand-new connection to the most important person in my life—myself. A new way of thinking about myself and about what was possible for me. It inspired me to create an entirely new way of experiencing life.

That's why I wrote this book.

It's time to cheer for YOU.

Ask yourself how you want to feel in every aspect of your life. Don't you want a high five life? A high five marriage, a high five job? Don't you want to be a high five parent and a high five friend? Don't you yearn to be seen and acknowledged and to feel the momentum of your strength and conviction pushing you forward?

Of course you do. That's what this book is all about: confidence and celebration of your SELF. With it, you can do or be anything. It ignites a chain reaction. It helps you create forward momentum, jump into celebration, forge a trusted connection with yourself, and bask in the high energy of joy.

The most powerful forces in the world are encouragement, celebration, and love. And you have withheld them from yourself. You're not the only one. We all do it.

Maybe you struggle to love yourself or can't change no matter how hard you try. Or maybe you're kicking ass and taking names, but can't truly enjoy life because you focus on what's wrong, not what's going right. Maybe your past is littered with horrible things that have been done to you, or horrible things you've done to other people.

No matter what's happened to you, I want you to see the truth.

You have a beautiful life right in front of you, and you can't see it. You have an incredible future that is just waiting for you to take control and create it. You have the most amazing ally, hype squad, and secret weapon staring at you in the mirror—and you ignore them. If you want to play a big game in life or just be happier, you must wake up and start treating yourself way better than you have been. It starts with that moment every morning, face-to-face with yourself in the mirror.

It starts with you.

If you want more celebration, validation, love, acceptance, and optimism, you must practice giving those things to yourself. For real. It starts with YOU. If you don't cheer for yourself and your dreams, who else will? If you can't look yourself in the mirror and see someone worth loving, why would anyone else? And speaking of everyone else: when you learn how to love yourself and support yourself, it helps every relationship in your life. When you can celebrate YOURSELF, it helps you cheer louder for others: your friends, your colleagues, your family, your neighbors, and your partner. That's because your relationship with yourself is the foundation of every relationship you have in life.

A word of warning.

At first, the high five will seem simple on its face, even stupid or weird. So humor me for a second, because there's a lot of research here.

The way it works on your subconscious mind and at a neural pathway level is deep. How it changes you lasts way longer than the handprints you'll leave all over your bathroom mirror. In the beginning, the high five is just something you do, but over time the validation, confidence, celebration, optimism, and action that it symbolizes becomes a part of who you are.

Here's the thing that's been a revelation to me: you can work hard, while being soft with your soul. You can take chances, screw up, and learn the lesson, without burying yourself in shame. You can have huge ambitions and still treat yourself and others with gentle kindness. You can face really hard and terrible situations in life and double down on optimism, resilience, and faith to get you through. When you stop making yourself wrong for how you're feeling, you'll immediately feel better.

It's only when you learn how to cheer, encourage, and support yourself through the ups and downs, that you'll naturally stop struggling and life will start flowing in the direction that is meant for you. You have no idea how much easier things could be if you stopped being so hard on yourself. How much more beautiful life could be. How much more rewarding the highs would become if you aren't constantly taking yourself so damn mentally low.

You deserve to be celebrated.

Not a year from now. Not when you get that promotion or lose that weight or achieve that goal. You deserve to be cheered for, as you are, where you are, right now, starting today. You not only deserve it—you need it. It satisfies your most fundamental emotional needs: to be seen, heard, and acknowledged. More than that, based on research, you thrive when you receive this kind of support. Feeling encouragement, believed in, and celebrated are the most inspiring forces on the planet.

That's why I believe your daily life should be infused with habits of celebration and optimism. By intentionally and deliberately cheering for yourself just for waking up, starting your day, and developing the habits to keep supporting yourself *no matter what*, you can burst through every single thing that's holding you back, change your life, and achieve your own personal fulfillment.

After a few weeks of high fiving myself in the mirror, I knew this simple habit was changing me in profound ways. I no longer focused on the things I thought I hated about myself. I began to realize the LEAST interesting thing about me is how I look. The best part and most lovable part is what's on the inside.

What happened to me will happen to you, too.

When you make high fiving yourself a daily habit, you will discover the secret to self-love and self-acceptance. This is another weird part about high fiving yourself: you stop seeing the physical you and you see the YOU within. The person and all that your life represents.

You're not just seeing your physical self in the mirror—you are greeting your presence, like a neighbor waving to you from their front porch. You raise your hand and silently say to yourself, *Hey you! I see you! You got this. Let's do this,* every morning. All of this will have a major impact on your mood, your feelings, your motivation, your resilience, and your attitude.

Before the High 5 Habit, I used to start my day feeling like I was pushing a boulder up a hill. Now I was leaving my bathroom every morning feeling the wind at my back.

Each day, as I raised my hand to my reflection, that connection with myself grew stronger.

In fact, it felt so good that one day, I snapped a picture of myself doing it and posted the photo on social media. You know, because that's what we influencers do. We share the love. I did not write a caption or an explanation. Not even a hashtag. I just posted the image to my Instagram story of me high fiving myself in my bathroom mirror and went on with my day.

Turns out, I'm not the only one on the planet who needed a high five that day.

CHAPTER 2

Science Says This Works

Here's that very first high five I shared on social media.

Notice, there are no instructions. Just me, standing there, thankfully in more than my underwear. My retainer still in. My bed head intact. Giving myself a high five in the mirror.

In less than an hour, people around the world started tagging me in photos of themselves high fiving the mirror. I was stunned—men, women, children, grandparents; before work, before school, before the day started—people of all ages and backgrounds were taking a moment to celebrate themselves in the mirror.

That was day one.

Little did I know how fast the High 5 Habit would spread, or how it would change so many people's lives by changing how they see themselves.

Here are a few of those photos from the first few days:

Science Says This Works

Hustle.
YOU can do it

YOU DESERVE A HIGH FIVE
EVEN ON THE HARD DAYS 🤍

Even when you are
🛁 still high 5
yourself.
You are alive and
doing life!

gosia_adamczyk_kaemka
Świętokrzyskie Voivodeship

EE ME, I
AYED

@MELROBBINS

85 likes

gosia_adamczyk_kaemka Zasada jest prosta - słuchać i ćwiczyć nawyki osób, które swoją mądrością zmieniają świat innych. To wymaga oczywiście pracy nad sobą i samodyscypliny, ale jeśli wiedzisz, że te małe nawyki każdego dnia przybliżają Cię do Twojego większego celu - determinacja cały czas rośnie.

another bathroom
high five

headed out to do the
grocery shopping for the
week...
but FIRST!
@MELROBBINS

rhet_eric

12 likes

Just look at the images for a minute. There is an energy and enthusiasm in everyone who tries it. In one of these images, the person you see high fiving themselves is in a bathroom at a domestic violence shelter. It is a powerful reminder that no matter where you are, what you are facing, or how little or much you have, you still have you. A high five costs nothing and what it gives you is priceless: a moment of validation. It is proof that you are still standing, still smiling, and that no matter what happens today, YOU have your own back. I loved seeing all these photos because it made me think maybe this high five thing isn't so cheesy after all. And then, it dawned on me: maybe it's not just me who needs one every day.

This is big. You may want to take notes.

So, I did what I always do when I want to understand something—I started digging for answers. Why is something so simple so damn powerful and contagious?

First stop: I reached out to people who had tagged me in their high five photos online. Those initial conversations confirmed a really cool thing that was happening for us all: when you give yourself a high five, it is impossible to think something crappy about yourself.

Try it—it's true.

When you look at yourself in the mirror and raise your hand in celebration, you cannot think: God, I look fat. I'm a loser. I am a horrible person. I hate my stomach. It's impossible. I tried to say "I hate my neck" out loud as I touched the mirror. You can't do it. I just laughed as the words came out. It is impossible to have a negative thought because for your entire lifetime, you have had a positive association with giving someone else a high five. As soon as you raise your hand to high five yourself, your subconscious mind flips into a positive mode and silences the critic in your head.

It's also impossible to high five yourself while worrying about your to-do list, or a work email, or something you have to do today. That's because a high five is a gut check for RIGHT NOW. It snaps you into the present moment. Think about it, there's nothing worse than receiving or giving a high five that feels limp or misses the full contact of your hand. To give a good one, you've got to concentrate on the action and *the intention.* You must be fully present. The same thing happens when you give one to yourself.

And that habit of worrying that normally hijacks you when you start brushing your teeth—*How am I going to finish that presentation in time and get my mom to her doctor's appointment?*—gets silenced by the act of raising up your hand. The mental death spiral ends and the focus begins: *I see you. I believe in you. I am here with you. You got this.*

The High 5 Habit is not a gesture—it is SELF-validation.

I don't care if you are standing in your boxer shorts, a ratty robe, your exercise gear, or your birthday suit. When your hand slaps the mirror, you feel seen, heard, and appreciated.

Plus, as soon as your hand hits that mirror, your mood isn't the only thing that's shifted. Your perspective gets a shift too. It makes you think about what bigger game you want to play today. Right now, you stand in front of the mirror and you mindlessly march through your to-do list—which is why you tank mentally. You start focusing on everyone and everything else. When you practice the high five, you think about what you want to do for yourself. How do you want to show up today? Who do you want to be? What is the one personal project that you need to make some progress on for yourself?

This moment of intentional reflection is more powerful than you think. Recent research from Harvard Business School has found that taking a moment to reflect on your work improves job performance, helps you be more effective, and makes you feel more motivated. It impacts everything from your confidence in achieving your goals to making you more productive. All from a simple moment of reflection.

As the months passed and I posted more about making the high five a habit, it began to rapidly spread around the world. Every day, I heard from people about the impact it was having and how they were teaching it to their co-workers, their kids, their friends, and their families. Companies took notice and began to ask me if I would speak to their teams about it.

Over the past year, I've presented the research and tools in this book to nearly half a million people in corporate speaking events around the world, and I am absolutely certain that this simple habit and the mindset tools in this book will change your life because it changes YOU.

Research backs it up.

The motivational power of a high five has been well documented. In fact, wait until you hear what researchers discovered about high fives when studying the best way to motivate kids in the face of challenging tasks. In one study, school-aged kids were split into three groups and asked to complete difficult tasks. Then, the researchers gave them one of three different forms of encouragement. The kids were either *praised for a trait* ("You're so smart." or "You're so talented."), or they were told they were working hard and *praised for their effort* ("You're really dedicated!"), or they were *simply given a high five.*

The high five was hands down the best motivator. Here's why: The kids who were told they were smart, talented, or skilled were the least motivated and had the least fun. Those praised for their effort showed greater enjoyment and exhibited a higher level of persistence. But kids who got a simple high five? They felt the most positive about themselves and their efforts, and they kept going for the longest time (persistence, people!), despite making mistakes. In fact, the results were so clear that the researchers titled the study "High Fives Motivate" when they published it in the academic journal *Frontiers in Psychology.*

Researchers concluded that giving a high five to someone is a *shared celebration.* Holding up your hand with a big smile on your face are two instantly recognizable signs of genuine pride and encouragement. A high five means you are celebrating WITH the other person. You are passing your energy on to them. That is so different from offering passive verbal praise. When you get a high five, you are seen and affirmed as a person. Not for your skills, your effort, or your grades. You are being praised and recognized just for being YOU. And what I am telling you is you can tap into that same power when you can give that high five to yourself in the mirror. And here's something else to consider: you don't have to say a thing. The high five itself communicates celebration and belief.

Repeating mantras and statements like "I love myself" can be powerful, but research proves that unless you actually BELIEVE the mantra you're saying, your mind will find reasons to reject it. (In Chapter 7, you'll learn how to create "meaningful mantras"— which are positive statements your mind embraces.) This is also why a high five is so amazing. Your mind doesn't reject it because it's always associated the high five with believing in the person you're giving it to. Plus, a high five isn't passive verbal praise. When you give yourself a high five, you prove to your brain, "I'm the kind of person who cheers for themselves." It's a physical act of *joining in with yourself*, acknowledging yourself, and trusting yourself.

As Brigid found when she started practicing this habit each day, "It's one thing to say positive things to yourself in your mind, but another to act that feeling out! It gives it more meaning, bolsters that action to help you truly believe in yourself and your worth. As they say, actions speak louder than words!"

High fives, trust, and how to build champions.

A high five also helps you build trust in yourself and your ability to win in life. UC Berkeley researchers studied NBA players' habits of success. At the beginning of a season, they recorded how often players gave each other high fives and other signs of encouragement, like fist bumps. Using the number of high fives during a game at the beginning of the season, the researchers then predicted which teams would have the best records at the end of the season.

The best NBA teams—those who made it to the championships—were the ones who gave the most high fives at the start of the season. Why are high fives such good predictors of a positive outcome? It comes down to trust. The teams who high fived constantly lifted each other up. The physical touch says, *I've got your back. Let's go, we've got this.* It helps you shake off a bad play. It lifts your mood. It communicates confidence. And reminds you that you can still win.

The high five teams believed in each other and in their ability, as a team, to win. They played like they trusted each other. The unspoken power they shared helped them become unstoppable. Conversely, the worst teams in the NBA barely touched. They had terrible body language. No high fives. Nada. And it showed: they consistently made selfish, inefficient plays, and their records reflected it.

Even if a team has good players, that's not enough. When you are high fived through every moment of practice, through the whole season, and right to winning a championship. It creates a culture of celebration and encouragement. It makes you selflessly give it your all. That's the feeling you need, and you can create that partnership with yourself.

Crushing your business goals as a team.

This high five is not just for sports. We need to be seen, supported, and celebrated at work too. Just look at research from Google. They conducted a three-year study called "Project Aristotle," which set out to determine what makes for the best teams. The finding was the same: the high-performing teams, in work and in life, are ones where every team member feels seen, heard, and can trust their teammates. The best teams create "psychological safety." Feeling like other people have your back and will cheer you on makes you more resilient and optimistic. It creates an atmosphere of trust and respect.

And, to take it a layer deeper, research also shows that the single biggest difference in whether or not you enjoy your job and find your work meaningful is not the quality of what you're producing or the number of vacation days you get or even how much you're paid. The lynchpin to your happiness at work is whether or not you have a manager who cares about you. A high five manager has your back and is someone you can trust—and who trusts you. When you walk into work, you want to feel like you matter. You feel seen and appreciated.

A high five in the mirror communicates those exact things— to yourself! If a good day at work is about being appreciated, doesn't it make sense to start every day by appreciating yourself? Of course it does!

Think that was convincing? Read THIS.

Okay, all that research explains why a high five feels so motivating and empowering, but it doesn't end there. I'm not going to ask you to high five yourself every morning in the mirror in your underwear and tell you it's going to change your life, unless I really know it's going to make a difference. I wanted to understand how a high five changes your brain at a structural level, because that's what I was experiencing. Over time, my mind stopped focusing on my "flaws" out of habit. I was able to just accept myself as I am.

For answers, I started with a body of research called "neurobics." Discovered by Dr. Lawrence Katz, a neurobiologist and researcher at Duke University, neurobic interventions are one of the easiest, most powerful ways to create new pathways and connections in your brain. In a neurobic exercise, a routine activity (*let's say, looking at yourself in the mirror*) is paired with two things: (1) something unexpected that involves your senses (*like high fiving that mirror*) and (2) an emotion you'd like to feel (*like celebration*).

Neurobic exercises make your brain snap into attention. The act creates a kind of "brain fertilizer" that makes your brain learn new habits faster. This heightened state creates new nerve connections in your brain that connect the action—which was once something routine (*high fiving other people*), but when done in an unexpected way (*high fiving yourself*), puts your brain on alert—with the emotion you'd like to feel.

For example, studies have found that brushing your teeth with your nondominant hand while repeating a thought forces your brain to pay extra close attention to that message. Using your nondominant hand makes your brain focus, so it zones in on everything that's happening—including what you're saying while you're brushing your teeth. This effort makes you accurately remember the words and the feelings they evoke, because you paired it with this new physical habit (*brushing your teeth with the wrong hand*).

The high five works in a similar way: When you high five your-self in the mirror (*something you don't normally do*), your brain pays attention. Thanks to the decades of positive associations with a high five, your brain begins to marry that positive association with the image of yourself. Our brains like to rely on mental shortcuts like this, which is why the High 5 Habit is the fastest and easiest way to override your pattern of looking at yourself and feeling self-doubt and self-hatred, and replacing it with the feeling of self-love and self-acceptance.

MIT, High Fives, and Dyslexia.

I soon realized I'd already seen the power of neurobics in our son, Oakley. In the fourth grade, we figured out that he has dyslexia and dysgraphia, which are language-based learning differences, and enrolled him in a school that specializes in language-based learning called the Carroll School. I sat in on a tutoring session once where the teacher explained to me that the school was part of an ongoing research program with an MIT neuroscience lab. The interventions they were doing with dyslexic students were designed to stimulate new neural pathway development.

Part of the challenge with being dyslexic is that many of the neural pathways that connect one side of the brain to another aren't formed yet. Literally, it's just gray matter. The school used neurobic intervention to stimulate new neural pathways and men-tal flexibility. I think about it like jumping a car. The wiring is there in your brain—it just needs a little neurobic spark to fire up.

The school had a gigantic board covered in little lights and a line down the middle. Whenever one of the lights lit up, Oakley was asked to touch it. Here's the catch: he had to use his left hand to touch the lights on the right side, and he had to use the right hand to touch the things on the left side. Combining the thought, *Touch it on the right side,* with the physical action of moving your arm to the opposite side, forges mental dexterity. It literally changed the structure of his brain, making new neural pathways, just like plowing a driveway in the snow.

The High 5 Habit is similar. As you learned a moment ago, when you combine moving your arm in an unusual way (*high fiving your-self in the mirror*), you're doing something different, which requires your brain to pay close attention. Plus, you have a lifelong, positive association with giving and receiving high fives. Your subconscious is programmed to associate celebration, belief, and possibility with a high five. So when you raise your hand to your own reflection, your subconscious says, "I am someone who is worth celebrating, believing in, and I can make anything happen."

The more you repeat the behavior, the more your brain associates confidence and celebration with your own reflection. It gradually flips your default opinion of yourself from negative to positive. At the same time, you reprogram your subconscious to stop criticizing your reflection and start loving it.

We need to talk about the story you tell yourself.

At this point, I was convinced that the high five in the mirror was creating new neural pathways helping me strengthen my self-esteem, self-worth, and self-confidence, but I still wanted to make sure. So, I called one of the world's leading experts in how the brain learns new information and habits, neuroscientist Dr. Judy Willis. I told her about how the High 5 Habit had made a profound difference in my life—and how it was working for hundreds of people I had spoken to while researching this book.

She explained how the brain can be changed. (And you'll learn more of her groundbreaking insights throughout the book—I can't wait for you to read Chapter 13 about how your nervous system impacts cognitive functioning and how to use your vagus nerve to your advantage.) She agreed that with this simple practice I had indeed created a new, more positive automatic behavior, belief, and new neural pathways in my mind. If I can do it, so can you.

This validation of the High 5 Habit is critical because as you will learn in Chapters 4–6, whatever you think, over and over, becomes your default subconscious belief. For years, that default of yours has probably been something awful—*I'm not good enough, nothing works out for me, I always screw everything up, why bother, God I'm ugly.* Mine (as you'll soon learn) is that everything is my fault and someone is always mad at me. You are going to learn how to use the High 5 Habit to reprogram that default belief. Because more than anything, you need to learn how to be kind to yourself.

Be kind. Be kind. Be kind.

So one final piece of research: When researchers study all the things that you could change in your life that make a meaningful impact on the quality of your life, the single most important change is making it a habit to be *kind to yourself.*

Researchers at the University of Hertfordshire in the UK did a study on things that create happiness and satisfaction. They looked at a whole range of behaviors and habits that you could do to improve your life, from exercising, to trying new things, to working on your relationships, to being kind to others, to doing things that bring you a sense of meaning, to working on your goals—you name it.

That study concluded that the number one predictor of how happy and satisfied you could be was self-acceptance. Meaning, how kind you were to yourself and how much you cheered for yourself had a direct and proportionate impact on your happiness. Being kind to yourself has the power to completely change your life—yet self-acceptance is what we practice the least. You'll drink the kale smoothie, go to the gym, get up earlier, cut out gluten, and meditate and the entire time beat yourself up about the fact that you're still not doing enough or not doing it right . . . That's why being kind to yourself is what really matters.

So why don't you do it?

None of us have been taught how. It's that simple. Our parents were hard on themselves so, in turn, they were hard on us. You may have grown up with a mom who criticized herself in the mirror or who felt guilty for taking time for herself. Or, a father who didn't express his emotions and measured his self-worth based on what he earned or how he achieved success outside the home.

If you're tough on yourself, blame the "tough love" you received as a child. Suck it up, pull your big girl pants up, wipe away those tears. My father hit me too, and I turned out okay. Honestly, that last one pisses me off. The worst parenting excuse in the world is "It was done to me and I'm okay." That makes zero sense to me. If you've suffered as a kid, you should do everything you can to make sure it doesn't happen to your kids. But that's not what happens. Your parents just repeated what was done to them.

That's why you're so tough on yourself. As a kid, your brain absorbed everything around you. That explains your unconscious drive to repeat some dynamics you learned as an infant and child.

Luckily, patterns are meant to be broken.

It's time to break this generational cycle. Not only does it feel awful to be hard on yourself, but research shows that when you're tough on yourself, it has the opposite impact that you want it to have. It is not motivating and it does not encourage you to achieve.

It just shuts you down. It makes you feel defeated and discouraged. It is the reason why you are stuck. To create a life of happiness and fulfillment, you need to be kinder to yourself—and that begins by practicing acts of kindness toward yourself every day.

Positive thinking isn't the answer.

If positive thinking alone changed your life, you would have already used it. I want to say something very loud and clear before we keep going. The High 5 Habit is not about fake praise or forced positive thinking. This is a book about changing the default programming that keeps you trapped in a destructive and unsupportive relationship with yourself.

You cannot think your way to a new life. You also can't wish your way to it. It's going to require you to practice some new habits. If you want your life to be different, you've got to start acting differently and making different decisions. While thinking positive thoughts can boost your mood, I know plenty of people who are still stuck no matter how much positivity they try to instill in their lives.

That's because the obstacles we face are real, and some of them are extreme.

You cannot look at a horrible situation and tell yourself that it's awesome. That's "toxic positivity" and you won't find any in this book. You can't gloss over serious problems, childhood traumas, systemic inequalities, addiction, racism, discrimination, chronic pain, abuse, and all the other enormously difficult experiences people face in their lifetimes. I spent years working as a criminal defense attorney at the Legal Aid Society and have seen firsthand how poverty and systemic discrimination push people off their intended paths.

Life can be cruel and unfair at times. Whether your problems are merely annoying, or the kind that crush your soul and spirit, they are real and they are in your way. No one knows what it's like to be in your shoes but you. That's why you must practice being kind to yourself and giving yourself the love, support, and celebration you need. You have the power to face these problems and change your life. You can't change what happened, but you can choose what happens next. That's where your true power is.

No matter how atrocious your past was, you can create a different future. It doesn't matter that your habits are self-destructive or that your mistakes have been disastrous. You can change what happens next. Know that no matter how deep your pit of shame may be, you can climb out of it and start over.

High fiving yourself won't change any of those things that have happened or the very real challenges you are facing right now. It changes YOU. It makes you better equipped to face the circumstances of life—whether you're waking up in a shelter, or the first day after a breakup, or the day after being fired, or maybe on the morning of your 5th round of chemo, like Jenn:

Jenn Reasinger
Not in the mirror, but high 5 for my 5th round of chemo. One more round to go!

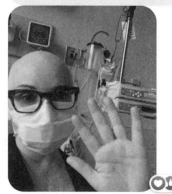

Jenn said, "Keeping the right mental attitude is 99% of the battle to getting through cancer and getting through chemo. I'm always concerned about everyone else and pulling everybody else up and encouraging them and we forget to encourage ourselves sometimes. That's why I love just looking in the mirror and giving myself a high five and being like, *You can do it.* This round of chemo I'm going through has been kind of kicking my ass a bit. So I go and give myself a high five to encourage myself. To be my own cheerleader. It's how I'm taking control and being that positive light in my own life to move forward."

Still need convincing? Do it anyway.

At this point, I sound like a broken record, but that brings me back to the mirror. Making it a habit to see yourself every morning and raise your hand in celebration of YOURSELF is the first step in building a new relationship with yourself. It's the most important relationship you have. It shapes every other relationship and the decisions you make. When you replace that self-doubt and self-criticism that drags you down with self-acceptance and self-love that lifts you up, your life will change.

So, how about YOU make this a habit?

CHAPTER 3

I Have a Few Questions . . .

Q: How exactly do I start doing it?

It's very simple.

Every morning, before you look at your phone or let the world in, take a moment to be with your reflection. The second you leave that bathroom, almost every moment is going to be about other people. You'll be distracted by your phone, what's going on at work, or what your kids need. The High 5 Habit is a moment every morning for you. It has two simple, but powerful, steps:

1. *Standing in front of the mirror, just be with yourself for a second.*

Don't focus on your appearance. Go deeper. See the person who is inside that body. The spirit beneath the skin and the soul behind that face.

2. *When you feel ready, high five yourself in the mirror.*

Notice how your mind goes quiet. You might feel a boost of energy. You might feel a sense of comfort: *It'll be okay.* You might think, *I got this.* It's a powerful moment. Without saying a word you're telling yourself, *I love you. I see you. I believe in you. Let's go.* Don't rush it. Revel in it. This moment is for you.

Q: Why do it first thing in the morning?

There are two reasons to make it the start of your day:

1. *It will impact your productivity and how you show up all day.*

When you high five yourself first thing in the morning, you set a positive tone for your day—and research shows your mood in the morning impacts your productivity for the rest of the day. You may be surprised by the shift. Caroline told me that she was amazed by how "weirdly motivated" she felt all day after doing the high five.

Or like Gloria, you may find that the high five creates an infectious energy that stays with you all day. She wrote, "I was a cheerleader in high school, so I chanted an old cheer—and then fell on the floor laughing like a crazy lady. I am 76 years young! I FEEL GOOD!"

Niki felt it too: "I just walked by the mirror and high-fived myself! I felt a little silly, and then I literally laughed out loud. I said 'You go girl!' And went about my way. What a feeling—I feel unstoppable. I'm on my wayyyyyyyyyyy!!! And now it feels like, 'Who's coming too?'"

Start the day in a positive state and you're more likely to take action. And action is the secret. You can't think your way to a new life. You must take the steps to create it. Basically, the high five sets you in motion to take control of your life.

2. *It teaches you to put your own needs first—from the moment you wake up.*

I love this insight that Nina shared with me: "How is it that I'm able to encourage others all day long, and yet don't take the time to encourage myself? In fact, I just now shared this with a friend: *'You are enough all on your own!!! You are beautiful, unique, and creative— learn to love and embrace YOURSELF!'* And . . . wouldn't you know . . . THAT is the very thing I, I, I, ME—that I needed to hear! It made me realize, I put others before me."

Instead of getting up and looking at social media, or emails, or taking care of everyone else— just take a moment and give that same love, support, and attention to yourself. As Nina said, "It's time to go look in the mirror and give myself that pep talk and a high five for being so awesome."

Q: Do I have to touch the mirror? I don't want to smudge it!

You can do this however YOU want. Touch the mirror or don't touch it. Give a high five or low five. Spread your fingers or keep your fingers together. It doesn't matter how you do it. Just make sure you do it.

Q: Why do you high five in the bathroom?

The bathroom is one of the few places you're bound to be alone and face-to-face with yourself. If you're at the gym, at work, or at school, you'll probably feel too self-conscious to try it. Plus, you already have a routine every morning when you stand in front of that mirror, so just add in your high five to your routine. Research shows that when you "stack," or pair a new habit (*high five*) with an old one (*brushing teeth*), you are more likely to do it.

One mindfulness trick I love is to mentally "be where my feet are." As you fix your hair, shave your beard, or apply your makeup, don't drift into autopilot. Take a moment to pause and actually be with yourself. An intentional glance in the bathroom mirror is meaningful. It can be an intimate moment of self-recognition, appreciation . . . even love. It can be your ONE chance ALL day to acknowledge your own strength, beauty, and fabulousness. But it rarely is—until now.

Q: Does it have to be in the mirror, or can I just high five my hands together in the air?

That is not a high five. That's an awkward clap.

The mirror is required! The science explains why: You are fusing the positive association that your brain has with a high five (*I believe in you!*) with your reflection. This habit is the beginning of a beautiful new partnership with yourself. You have lost a piece of yourself in the busyness of life. I know I sure have. This morning high five is the fastest way to become more connected to yourself, your needs, your goals, your dreams, and the greater forces around you.

Q: Why is it called the High 5 Habit?

Habit is just a fancy word for "pattern." Habits are easy to learn when you turn them into small, simple things you practice every day. The high five feels so good, you'll find it's an easy habit to remember and repeat.

I call it a habit and not the Morning High 5 because a habit must be repeated in order to become second nature. You are making the mistake of waiting to feel worthy of self-love and celebration. Let's change that by making it a habit.

In fact, it will quickly become second nature, like it has for Dominique, who said, "I woke up in the middle of the night to let my dog out. I was walking by a mirror, stopped, high fived myself and went back to sleep. The High 5 Habit has already become part of my life, even half asleep!" And the more high fives you do, the more you find yourself loving the habit itself—which also means you are in love with the process of learning to love yourself again!

Q: Does it work for everyone?

Absolutely.

But you have to do it. It won't work if you do it for two days and then tell everybody it's stupid. All habits require repetition (see my rant, above). Habits can be hard in the beginning because you're not used to doing them yet. You'll feel like quitting before it becomes something that sticks. Change is simple, but it's not always easy, *and* you can do it if you force yourself to practice it every morning in the mirror.

Lisa and her daughter felt it working right away: "I started this with my 9-year-old daughter today. She said it made her feel so good. She was grinning ear to ear. I love how much positivity comes from such a simple act!" Repeat the act over and over again and you are building the confidence to create a more positive life.

Q: Why not high five someone else?

You already high five everybody else.

You spend too much of your time seeing everything and every-body else, absorbing what *they* want, what *they* need, what *they* expect. This is why you're last on your list. That's also why you carefully manage your appearance, your facial expressions, and your reactions to meet the external gaze of those around you. You think your self-worth and self-esteem are reflected back by how other people perceive you. If they like you, or if they think you are smart, worthy, or good enough, THEN you feel smart, worthy, and good enough.

You're looking in the wrong mirror when you look for your worth in other people's approval. A million likes on social media means nothing if you don't like yourself. Flip the focus from exter-nal validation—Likes. Follows. Views. Praise—to giving that val-idation to yourself, just for being alive and standing here ready to seize the day.

Q: I'm really surprised by how emotional it made me. Is this normal?

Yes. It's really, really normal. In fact, many people who try it are surprised by the emotions that come up. You might relate to some of these stories:

Alyssa said, "I high-fived myself in the mirror yesterday. I didn't think anything would happen, but I started crying out of nowhere. My soul had been waiting on that forever. #INeededThat."

Wendy shared that after starting to do this habit, she initially felt exhausted. That night she found herself in bed early and overcome with emotion. But the next morning, she woke up energized and suddenly able to get done a bunch of tasks she had been putting off. She said, "I think maybe I released some blocks." If this happens for you too, that's normal.

Sometimes the emotional release you feel may be really positive. Michael said, "I did a high five in the mirror and it felt amazing . . . I made myself blush!" and Jeannette told me that she can't help but jump in the air after her high five. Whatever your reaction, allow yourself to feel it.

Q: Why does something so simple work?

The genius and power of this habit is precisely *because* it's so simple.

It would be easy to think this is the stupidest thing you've ever heard. But therein lies the secret: if it's simple, you'll do it. Tools only work when you use them. Behavior change only happens when you repeat the behavior. Research shows us that to build a new habit, it needs to be easy to add to your routine. Since it's easy and it feels really good, by doing it each day, you'll prove to yourself that you can stick to a challenge, and that's what builds confidence.

Q: Why should I trust you?

You don't have to. I'm trying to teach you how to trust yourself. I don't want you to look at me. I'm turning you back toward the reflection in the mirror.

Q: I've got real problems, Mel. How can this help me during the tough times?

As you heard from Jenn in the last chapter, high fiving herself doesn't cure her cancer. But it does help her feel encouraged, supported, and celebrates her strength as she fights the cancer. The same goes for any difficulty you're facing: you need to high five yourself through it.

Lauryn wrote, "I'm a single mom. In the past year, I lost one of my very closest friends to suicide as well as walking away from a relationship that was not good for me. I struggled with feelings of sadness, feelings of being unsuccessful, and not enough. Every time I see a mirror, I now give myself a high five. I do it to remind myself that I am alive and worthy to get out there to grab my dreams . . . mostly to inspire my daughters to live their lives happily, with authenticity, to know that they are enough no matter what life throws at them."

Or maybe you're dealing with something at work. Kendra said, "My company hasn't been netting sales, but I still high-five myself daily to stay encouraged." And Breanne wrote, "I finished a project today I have been working on and struggling through for a month. As I looked at my final product, I was amazed and proud of my work! I handed the project over with my head held high and a smile on my face. The feedback I got: 'It's ok, it's a start.' Typically, I would spend the rest of this day bashing myself, doubting myself, overthinking, shutting down. Not this time. Something in me forced me to go to the mirror, high five myself, and now I am rewarding my hard work with some me-time today."

Like those kids who do the high five in that research study, in the face of failure and challenge, that encouragement and partnership with yourself is exactly what you need! The high five reminds you that you can face whatever it is that you're going through. And it reminds you that you have the resilience, the stamina, the strength, and the courage to meet this moment in your life, and to come out on the other side. That high five acknowledges how hard you are working. Just as a teammate would support you in the biggest play of your life, you can support yourself with a daily high five that says, *You can handle this. I know you can.*

Q: What if I don't feel like doing it?

Do it anyway. Part of the reason why you don't have what you want in your life is because when you don't feel like doing it, you don't do it. Your life only gets easier when you do the hard things all the time. Push through your resignation and do it.

Read what Paula had to say after she started doing the high five. Her realization is heartbreaking, and I think it's also a very common reason people don't feel like doing it, which is why I wanted to share it with you:

"It's hard for me to cheer for myself because I resent anyone with the audacity to love themselves. It sounds crazy, but it's like, *Will I be likable if I like myself? Aren't women who tout their achievements bitches?* I hate women who constantly tout themselves, but they are also the very people I admire. The founders, the work-out-ers, the travelers.

I don't feel capable, not because my dreams are outlandish but because I feel like there are so many people who deserve it more, mostly because they'll cheer hard for themselves. So it's much easier to applaud the people who are ahead of me than it is to cheer for myself. It's easier to stay in the shadows than it is to go for gold and fall flat. It would be more proof that I am not good enough, and I have enough evidence of that."

When you read this quote, you can feel Paula's pain, and you can also feel her deepest desire. She wants to be seen and celebrated and to feel worthy. If holding yourself back is a habit, it's time to break it and learn how to start cheering yourself forward. Right now her dreams are haunting her. She longs to live a high five life. She wants to "go for gold." When you read this, you can see how your own thoughts can keep you stuck in a very low place. And when you cannot give what you desire to yourself, you will resent those who can. The high five is the first step to changing this.

Q: Isn't a high five only for when there's something to celebrate?

Absolutely not. Encouraging yourself every step of the way is the secret formula for winning in life. One of the most rewarding parts of running a road race is that people line up and cheer for you every step of the way. Learning how to do that for yourself, whether you cross the finish line or not, will build your confidence faster than any medal or accomplishment ever could.

Q: What if I feel like a failure right now?

If your self-esteem is in the gutter, then abso-freakin-lutely high five yourself. You need it right now. You deserve it. (And you've always needed it.)

Starting from the very first moment, your life has been a trial by fire. You answer a question wrong and everyone laughs. You speak your mind at the dinner table and get sent to your room. You try out for the football team and get cut. You think someone is a friend and they ditch you. You apply for a promotion and get passed over. You trust someone and they hurt you. You run for office and lose. You fall in love and get your heart broken. You start a business and it goes bankrupt. You achieve a dream and then start to feel lost again. And on and on and on.

You perceive these as failures, but they aren't. They're all lessons. Like steel, confidence, resilience, and wisdom are forged in fire. Your life is always teaching you something if you are willing to look at it that way. Why not reward yourself not only when you win but also when you fail spectacularly?! Until recently I had this reversed. I used to be the kind of person who held out on a reward until a goal was achieved, and I was hard on myself every step of the way.

What I've learned is that failures almost always lead to something amazing down the road. The High 5 Habit will help you pick yourself back up when it feels like life is knocking you down. And you need to, because you have the strength within you (and you're gonna need it) to knock right back when the time is right.

Q: Okay, I'm ready to start. What's the best way to begin and remember to do it?

I'm glad you asked because I've got your back to help you start.

TAKE THE High 5 Challenge

What is the High 5 Challenge? It's simple. For five days, start your day by high fiving yourself in the mirror. That's it. And here's the coolest part—you don't take this challenge alone. You and I will do the challenge together. Sign up for free at High5Challenge.com.

For 5 days, you'll be part of a global online community of people who are all doing the High 5 Challenge together. Every morning, I'll email you a link to a video pep talk that will inspire you and go even deeper into the research and the changes that you're going to experience. You'll be able to track your progress and connect with and cheer for other people who are doing the challenge with you. And even cooler, those same people are going to celebrate and cheer for you, too.

So while you may be alone in your bathroom when you high five yourself in the mirror, when you join us online at High5Challenge.com, you won't feel alone, because you aren't. And the best part? It's free, no strings attached. Just me, you, a ton of really positive people around the world, and your bathroom mirror.

Research tells us that it's a whole lot easier to change when you feel support and encouragement from other people. The fact is, you are not alone. People around the world are waking up every day and doing this with you. Take a minute and get registered for free right now.

High5Challenge.com

After just five days, you will be surprised by how different you feel. This is what Fran had to say: "I must say, it hits different every time I high five myself. I can feel something heal a little more. I believe a little more. This is day 5 of high fiving myself and being transformed by the renewal of my mind. Now, it's a movement. My friends and family started doing it as well. And now I see that I can make a profound difference in the world."

Q: Can it create lasting changes?

Yes. And the high five in the mirror is just the beginning. In the remainder of the book, you'll learn a dozen more ways to give yourself the encouragement and support you need. And as you practice using these tools to flip yourself from a place of being stuck into a state of taking action, you'll experience even cooler things related to confidence, happiness, and fulfillment.

Your relationship with yourself is the foundation for everything in your life. How you talk to and treat yourself sets the tone for everything you do. It determines how you feel, what you think, and what actions you take. If you look in the mirror and don't see a person worth celebrating, it's time to change that.

The bottom line is you have a lifetime of positive association with a high five because you've been doing it for strangers, friends, and teammates your entire life. By making it a habit to do it to yourself, it will change the patterns that are stored in your subconscious that relate to you—and that will improve your mood, help you achieve your goals, and fundamentally shift the trajectory of your life.

CHAPTER 4

Why Do I Torture Myself?

While I was writing this book, I received this text from one of our daughters.

> How do I not feel like the ugliest girl at the bar every time I go out?

It's the kind of text that breaks your heart because you know there isn't a damn thing you can say to change how she feels about herself at this moment in her life. Believe me, I've tried. I can tell her all the reasons why she's beautiful inside and out. I can remind her of her incredible character attributes. I can list her achievements and gush about her sense of humor, wisdom, and work ethic. I can compliment her for being a trusted, loving, and respected sister, friend, and colleague.

I can tell her all the cheesy things that authors, motivational speakers, and mothers say to someone they love who is single and feels discouraged: "You just haven't met someone who deserves someone as fantastic as you, yet . . . but you will."

Why walking on your hands is normal and loving yourself is not.

It doesn't matter what I think, because this text isn't about me. It shows you the relationship our daughter has with herself. How she sees herself, the world around her, and how she fits into it. I'm sure you've experienced this dynamic with someone you love. You see how amazing they are and gush about their talents, their attributes, and even their appearance. You try to convince them with facts. *That's not true. You do have friends. You are beautiful. You do have so much to offer!*

No matter what you say, or what evidence you use, it does not change what someone believes about themselves. They can hear it, it might make them feel better in the moment, but their brain flat out rejects it as truth. They've told themselves they suck so many times over the years and compiled so much evidence that it is true that this belief is now programmed into their subconscious mind. That's why the person you love will even argue with you when you tell them how great you think they are.

One of the most important revelations you can ever have is that your life and your happiness begins and ends inside your own mind. What you say to yourself, how you treat yourself, and the thoughts that run on repeat are everything. It does not matter how successful, thin, famous, muscular, or wealthy you become, if you always focus on what's "wrong" with you, you'll never be happy.

If you think there's something wrong with you, the idea of high fiving yourself in the mirror will sound "dumb," "stupid," or "cheesy" because you believe you aren't worthy of celebration until you've fixed what's "wrong." This is also why you feel uncomfortable when people compliment you. You don't believe it. That's why you can't accept it.

Celebrating yourself is about as foreign a concept as walking on your hands or eating with your feet. That's why your subconscious brain rejects it.

Your subconscious won't say I Love You.

Want to see your subconscious in action? Just look at yourself in a mirror or pay attention to what you do when someone tries to take your picture.

My kids used to tease me because every time I looked in a mirror, I made a "weird mirror face." I didn't even know I was doing it. Everybody has a mirror face. You look in the mirror and subconsciously see what you need to "fix" and then adjust your face to try to make it more attractive (why do we do this?!). If you don't realize you do it, just watch the teenagers in your life. They all have a mirror face: it's their "good side," or how they tilt their heads slightly, or suck in their cheeks when you try to take their photo.

My mirror face involves an ever so slight puckering of the lips—I only know this because my kids have teased me relentlessly about it. It's a subconscious reaction to my reflection to try to make myself look better. Well, I'm proud to say that I have not done the mirror face in at least three months because I don't actually look at my appearance anymore. I see ME, the person.

Here's what science tells us about mirror face: We all have automatic thoughts—things we think so often they become the default, like a rut in a path. If you deliberately change your actions or thoughts, you change your default way of thinking and acting. This deliberate change is called a "neuroplastic response." Right now, your default thinking—and mirror face—are making you hyper focus on what's wrong. The good news is, you can change that.

Something's wrong with you?

You don't need to know when or how you went from loving yourself to criticizing yourself. If you want to unpack where this belief started, give yourself the gift of working with a therapist. In our daughter's case, I asked her and she replied, "I don't know when it began, because I don't ever remember *not* feeling that way about myself or my body. And the truth is, I know I'm not that ugly. I am just the biggest one of all my friends. I hate it. And that's what I see in the mirror. I am bigger than I want to be, and it makes me feel horrible about myself." And then she said, "I wish I didn't think about it all the time. But I don't know how to stop."

And as we talked about it further, it was clear you can't hate your body and accept and love yourself at the same time. When you look in the mirror and focus on what you need to "fix," it's the opposite of a high five—it's self-rejection. She's not alone on this. According to research, approximately 91% of women are unhappy with their bodies, and the media and images that you are bombarded with don't help. When you constantly wish you looked different, or see a world reflected back in a way that makes you feel like you don't belong, your entire existence feels like something is wrong with you.

Here's why you must change your mind.

There are three reasons why you have to stop beating yourself up and learn how to love yourself and empower yourself.

1.   *When you focus on what's wrong, you will never change.*

With that attitude, every change you're trying to implement is a reminder that you need "fixing" and makes everything feel harder. This is why diets don't work—because exercise plans or diets feel like punishment. Being "on a diet" only reinforces the feeling that there is something wrong with you. That you're not okay or lovable or fantastic as you are.

2. *Hating your body, your past, or yourself won't motivate you.*

Research shows that beating ourselves up makes it harder to feel motivated. If you don't believe that you deserve to be celebrated or feel good, why on earth would you do the hard stuff it takes to change? You first must love and accept where you are, forgive yourself for whatever led you to this moment, and come from a place of self-love and self-worth: *I DESERVE to feel happier and healthier* and *I CAN take the steps to take better care of myself.* When you remind yourself that you're doing this because you love yourself, not because you hate yourself, that high five attitude will support you every step of the way.

3. *The more you repeat it, the more evidence you see.*

The relationship you have with yourself can set you free or keep you trapped. In the next chapter, you'll learn how these beliefs not only make you feel like crap, they change the filter in your brain and change the world you see in real time. Every day your mind is simultaneously spinning thoughts in your head about what's happening as it's happening. When things happen over and over, even if only in your mind, they wear a groove, a rut, in your brain. That groove becomes like a familiar path you ramble down. The same old scenery, the same twists and turns. You know it, and it knows you. It becomes part of who you perceive yourself to be. Telling all these stories to yourself turns a thought into a belief and over time into the identity you have about yourself.

You aren't to blame for the things you think. A lot of time, when you are critical of yourself, you learned it from a parental figure who was hard on themselves. Regardless of how you learned to beat yourself up, the bottom line is if it makes you miserable, you have a responsibility to change it.

The battle isn't with your body (or your bank account or your job).

The battle is with your self-hatred. You can't change from a place of hate. You must start from a place of love. And that's what the High 5 Habit helps. It teaches you how to see, speak, and treat yourself with loving kindness.

Nina did the five-day High 5 Challenge with me and had a powerful breakthrough: "I've been living with body dysmorphia for more than 20 years. After doing this for just five days, instead of hiding from my face, I'm finding myself grinning at me instead. Thank you."

Cathy said the High 5 Habit is fundamentally changing how she sees herself: "We have this pattern of seeing ourselves in the mirror and always looking at all the flaws. I notice my eyebrows are not aligned, my white hair is showing, gaaaah, why do I have a double chin now, my arms look flabby. I see so many things wrong with myself. And, in a world where Zoom and video calls and Facebook Lives rule, it's not just the mirror that we have to live with! It is seeing ourselves on the camera more times than we would want to. For me, the habit of high fiving myself in the mirror creates an affirmation, a physical act of celebrating myself. The act alone forces me to look at my face, my body in a different light: a brighter, kinder, more compassionate and joyful way. I've found I cannot high five myself and say bad things in the mirror!"

You deserve to be celebrated, as you are right now. Not when you lose the weight, make more money, fall in love, or get into graduate school. And research shows, when you learn how to love and accept yourself, you'll be better able to ride the ups and downs of life. You'll be more resilient. When you beat yourself up all day long, you're pounding yourself into the ground—and you're more vulnerable to feeling like you are being buried alive when life gets stressful. Everything becomes a beat down. When you start to look at yourself in the mirror and accept yourself as you are, right now, and see a person who deserves celebration and support, you'll tap back into that natural motivation, celebration, and resilience you were born with.

You weren't always like this.

Everything I'm about to teach you is already in you. Self-love is your birthright. As a baby, you loved the very sight of yourself. You'd crawl up to a mirror and you wouldn't just high five yourself. You'd press your face against your reflection, and smile and laugh and love on yourself, in one wet, sloppy, open-mouthed kiss. And there's so much about you to celebrate! Let's start with how unique and special you are. Your DNA sequence, your fingerprints, your voice, the patterns of your iris—every one of these things is entirely unique, and yours alone. How you see the world, the way you laugh, the things you experience, the way you love—it all comes together to create something magical. You are the only you that will ever exist. Each one of your distinctive gifts and talents is a phenomenon. You need to celebrate that shit.

And you are so much stronger than you give yourself credit for! Resilience is hardwired into your DNA. Think about when you learned to crawl as a baby. You didn't try once then give up. You didn't lay on the floor and gaze morosely at the ceiling and say, *Well I guess this is my life. It's time to throw in the towel. I will never crawl. I'll just live here, on this spot on the rug.* No, you tried again. And because you didn't have words, you couldn't tell yourself some sad story about how you just can't do it, you're not good enough, or smart enough, or strong enough. You kept trying and eventually you pulled yourself across the floor.

You are also naturally intelligent. By simply watching the people around you, you figured out how to coo, smile, crawl, scooch, and eventually walk. It didn't matter that you fell an average of 17 times an hour learning to walk. You. Just. Kept. Trying. That tenacity is still in you.

And celebration is part of your DNA too. As a kid, every time you succeeded at something thrilling and new, you'd laugh and screech and raise your arms up over your head. If the music would play, you'd shake your booty, wiggle, and jump around. You are perfectly designed to feel loved, resilient, joyous, and celebrated. That's why a stranger's high five feels so damn good. It strikes deep down to the core. It hits the YOU of you. It reminds you of something you've forgotten: who you really are and how you are meant to feel.

Wait, so what the heck happened to the happy me?

Simple, life got its hands on you. From an early age, your life stirred shit up. All the highs and the lows got tumbled together like a load of laundry in a dryer. Like I said, you were born perfect, whole, and complete and somewhere along the way, as you grew up, went to school, and tried to make friends and fit in, you got the message: *there's something wrong with you.*

The feeling that "there's something wrong with me" happens to everyone. Psychologists call it a "break in belonging." You start to feel like you don't belong in your family, your church, your friend group, your neighborhood, or the world at large. And that feeling then creates a second break in belonging—with yourself.

It can happen in a million different ways. Growing up, maybe you moved a lot and changed schools a few times, so you always felt like an outsider looking in. Maybe you were attacked or unsafe. Maybe you got labeled stupid because you were dyslexic and put in special classes. Or you were the only transgender person, the only Muslim, the only refugee, or the only Black kid in your class.

Maybe you got teased about how you looked, spoke, or acted. Or you felt uncomfortable getting undressed at gym class because your mom was constantly on you about your weight. When your home life, or friends at school, or the world itself makes you feel like you're not okay, or unsafe, or unworthy of love, as a kid, you believe it. It happens to all of us. No one gets to adulthood without experiencing this kind of trauma.

Maybe your father walked out on the family. Or Mom had severe depression. Or a brother died by suicide. Maybe you lived with constant worry about where your next meal was coming from. Maybe you experienced racism and bias every day in your neighborhood. Or your family rejected you because you were gay. Or a parent struggled with addiction or constantly shamed you with the silent treatment. These experiences impacted you. You absorbed them in your mind, body, and spirit. It's not like you could leave—you were just a kid. The only choice you had was to try to survive it.

This is especially hard on an emotional level.

When something happens to you as a kid, you don't have the life experience or the support system to process what's happening. You absorb it in your nervous system, coping patterns, and thoughts. Your only option is to do the best that you can to live through it. In a stressful, traumatic, or abusive situation, no child thinks, *These adults around me are seriously messed up.* Or, *Holy crap,* *this situation is f*cked.* Or, *This is illegal, I'm having you arrested.* Or, *If this kid is hurting me, I bet someone is hurting them.* Every child turns it back on themselves. They assume it's their fault.

That's what I did when I was molested at the age of nine by an older kid. I thought it was my fault. It's what our son did when he was relentlessly bullied at a summer camp. He hid his pain and blamed himself (and I still blame myself for not picking up the clues sooner and ripping him out of there).

I'm sure that's what you did too with the experiences you survived: you made it mean something terrible about you. Whether you were dealing with a critical mom, or parents who got divorced, or racist microaggressions every day, or physical abuse, you turned this on yourself. That is a massive flaw in human design. Instead of blaming the people who hurt you, you blame yourself and think, *There must be something wrong with ME.*

As much as I hate to admit it, as a parent, we often send that message unintentionally.

Try being the new kid with blue hair.

I'm about to tell you a story that I hate, because it makes me feel like a terrible mom. But I'm sharing it because it illustrates just how loud and consistent this message is—that *there's something wrong with who you are, what you look like, and how you express yourself.*

When our son, Oakley, was in the sixth grade he dyed the ends of his hair because he was a huge fan of the video gamer Ninja. It looked pretty cool and he loved it. Then he changed schools in seventh grade, and as we were leading up to the first day at his new school, I started to worry that kids might be mean to him if he showed up on day one with blue hair. It's hard enough to be the new kid in seventh grade. Try being the new kid with blue hair.

(*Actually, try being the new kid with blue hair, a neurotic mother, and her desperate need for you to fit in.*)

For weeks I kept asking him if he wanted to get a haircut before school, and maybe . . . cut off the blue tips? He wasn't nervous about it, but I was. As school got closer, his older sisters started to pile on: "You know, dude, it might not be the best thing to roll in with dyed hair. It's not like you're a star lacrosse player." Oakley caved and got a trim before his first day. He didn't do it for himself. He did it to appease our fears.

When you're a kid, everyone will tell you what to do, or what they'd like you to do. You acquiesce to make your mom happy, or fit in with the cool kids, or because you don't have a choice. It gets conditioned into you that love and acceptance are transactional. If you do what I say, then I'll love you.

Come to think of it, that's exactly why you withhold love from yourself, you learned to in childhood.

The bullsh*t we bought into.

Looking back on this story with our son, I realize the message I was sending was "There's something wrong with the way you look." I was also saying, *I'll only accept the version of you that makes me happy.* Yet in reality I felt the opposite. I loved his hair, but I didn't trust the other seventh graders would accept him with blue hair. I was trying to give him the best chance for a smooth, new start, but instead, I clearly made him question his own choices *and* whether or not I loved and accepted him exactly as he is.

I was telling him *I'd rather you fit in than be you.* I also feel horrible because I know this is core to a very big lie we believe: what other people think of you is more important than what you think of yourself. You bought into this bullsh*t your whole life because people you love taught you to believe it. Kids, if you are reading this, I'm really sorry.

God, I hate that story, but that's the heart of what happened to you, to me, to everyone you know. You started questioning what you look like, what you do, and ultimately, who you are.

It is how that connection to your truest self got blocked. It's why you stand in front of a mirror and pick yourself apart. For our daughter, or anyone who struggles with their appearance, you must start appreciating parts of yourself right now. Stop trashing yourself and just throw the jeans that don't fit into the trash. When you criticize yourself and beat yourself up, you are treating yourself the way I treated our son: your love for yourself is transactional. You are withholding it until you approve of you. It's a horrible way to go through your life.

Don't hate, appreciate.

You don't need to change anything to deserve the love and acceptance you need. You just need to start giving yourself that validation.

The next time you stand in front of a mirror, stop poking, prodding, and picking yourself apart. It's only making you feel defeated, rejected, and discouraged. And it sets the tone for what you think about and how you feel all day. Instead, start each morning looking for qualities that you appreciate about yourself. The little intricacies you ignore, your strength, and your intuition. How your body has taken care of you. Or how those stretch marks remind you of the kids you have.

SEE, THERE IS NOTHING WRONG WITH YOU. You may not be happy with where you are in life right now, the balance in your bank account, the number on the scale, the size of your pants. Lord knows it hasn't been easy, and yet, here you are. Still standing.

Resilient, intelligent, and strong. Still waking up every day and pushing yourself to learn and grow and become a better person. And honestly, that makes you f*cking awesome.

I love what Jordan shared with me after she started high fiving herself each morning: "So often self-love is shown to be about fixing yourself. That's why I love high fiving myself in the mirror, because it shows us that self-love is really about falling in love with the parts of yourself you've been trying to fix." There is so much about you to love. Soak it in. Then, raise your hand and seal this appreciation into your subconscious with a high five.

It's like you're missing something really big.

To understand the profound power of accepting and encouraging yourself, let's look at some more research on what psychologists call your core "fundamental emotional needs"—the things that all people need in order to thrive. In case you skipped (or slept through) the lecture in Psychology 101 on Maslow's Hierarchy of Needs, here's the background: we all have basic needs that are fundamental to our fulfillment, happiness, and survival.

You know that you need water, food, oxygen, shelter, and sleep, or you'll die. You also know that you need friendship, or else you'll feel lonely and research shows that loneliness can kill you too. You may also know that you have a fundamental need to grow as a person, and when you don't, you feel stuck.

But you may not know that you have three core emotional needs: to be seen, heard, and loved for the unique individual that you are. When those emotional needs aren't met, it's not only a form of neglect, but you will feel unloved, invisible, and unfulfilled. I believe that's how we all got so self-critical in the first place. And we've been twisting ourselves in knots ever since.

You can change this for yourself.

What is missing is a deeper connection to yourself. You have been so busy running from one thing to the next, that you can't grasp right now how big of a shift it will create when you start each morning by honoring yourself. A high five fulfills the deepest and most important emotional needs that are central to every human's well-being.

As you've learned, often these three emotional needs were never met during your childhood, and you haven't been given the tools (until now) to fulfill them as an adult. It is the reason why you feel invisible at work, on the outside of your friend group, and disconnected in your relationships as adults—not to mention to yourself. There's something missing: a deeper sense that you matter. This desire to be seen, heard, and appreciated is critical to being fulfilled as a human being.

Don't bother arguing with me: I did the math.

First of all, your very existence is so miraculous you should feel seen and celebrated! First, the odds of you being born are one in a million because your mom carries over one million eggs during her lifetime. Crazy, but that's not even close to the mathematical phenomenon you are. Based on recent research, scientists have figured out that the egg that formed you was choosy and could determine which of your father's 250 million sperm cells it wanted to connect with. If the egg that created you chose any other sperm, your sibling would be holding this book because you never would have been born.

Experts had put the odds of YOU being the result of that sperm and egg encounter, at 1 in 400 trillion. And even that isn't accurate. A scientist from Harvard wrote a research paper about the odds of you being born and the number is so insane, it looks like this: 1 in I don't even know how to say that number. It proves that the odds of YOU being born are nothing short of a miracle.

Someone as unique and special as you deserves to be seen, heard, and celebrated. Feeling like you matter, that someone cares about you, and that you are worth celebrating are your most fundamental and important emotional needs. They are as important to your well-being and happiness as food and water. The difference between a good day and a bad day can sometimes come down to just being acknowledged by someone. And you know who is the best person to validate you? YOU. And that brings me back to that moment every single morning when you come face-to-face with yourself in the mirror.

High fiving yourself is so much more than a physical act. It is foundational. It's a transfer of energy. It symbolizes an alliance and an unwavering belief in yourself and your ability. You aren't congratulating yourself. You are celebrating yourself as you are. Your existence makes you worthy of a high five. Your presence, your hopes, your dreams, your capacity to love, your ability to heal, to change, to grow, your heart, your soul—that's what makes you worthy of being celebrated.

When you high five yourself in the mirror, you are fulfilling those fundamental emotional needs for yourself. You see yourself. You hear yourself saying, "It'll be okay" or "You can do it" or just "I love you." All the things you've been wishing your parents, your friends, your spouse, or your boss would communicate, you give to yourself in that one action that communicates:

Confidence—I believe in YOU.

Celebration—YOU are amazing.

Validation—I see YOU.

Optimism—You CAN do this.

Action—YOU got this, keep going.

Wouldn't it be incredible to feel all those feelings at once? The world would explode with puppies and rainbows and unlimited data for everyone. (*What? Don't act like you're not getting killed by overages too.*) It would be mind-blowing. Literally. It could possibly blow up your subconscious because it's not programmed to absorb all that yummy, gooey love from you . . . yet. But it will be . . . and now that you know that self-validation, self-love, and self-acceptance are the most powerful motivating forces in the world, I know what you are thinking . . .

Okay, I get it, but how do you think different thoughts?

The first step is catching the old thought that takes you low.

If you don't know what it is, here's a hint: It's some version of *I'm not _____ enough.*

You can fill in the blank with anything you want. Go ahead, pick your poison: I'm not smart enough, good enough, tall enough, skinny enough, rich enough, successful enough, talented enough, light enough . . . whatever it is you're not enough. I call it poison because thinking it is like drinking it. It kills your spirit and your innate desire to be seen, heard, and celebrated.

This thought is the exact opposite of the validation, confidence, celebration, optimism, and action that a high five symbolizes. It takes you mentally LOW. The thought alone can paralyze your ability to move forward. Here's a big one: When you think this thought, you don't feel like high fiving anyone or anything. Especially yourself.

Why would you? Let's change that.

CHAPTER 5

Am I Broken?

The other night, we were having a family dinner and one of our daughters started talking about friction she was having with one of her roommates.

"I just always feel like I'm the bad guy. It doesn't matter what I say, or how I say it. Every time I talk about what's bothering me or express a boundary, I end up feeling like I am in the wrong. It's happened so many times, I'm always telling myself, *I'm selfish. I'm a bad person.* That has been my entire year. I don't know how to stop feeling this way about myself."

My husband, Chris, tried to console her: "You're not a bad person. Maybe you've done bad things, but you're not a bad person. Everyone screws up. That's how you learn. Just promise me that you will stop telling yourself you are a bad person." And then he went on to explain that "after the restaurant business collapsed, I felt like a complete failure. My business partner viewed it as the risk that goes with opening a restaurant. I couldn't. I made it mean that I was a failure. Everywhere I looked, that's what I saw. I wasn't there enough for you kids. I failed at being a good husband to your mom. I hadn't made enough money. I couldn't do anything right. If you keep repeating it, you'll believe it. Shame is like a pair of dark sunglasses. It colors everything you see."

She said, "Well, I have that story too, Dad. Being a music student, I walk into a classroom or a studio and I always notice how much more talented and cool other people are. I think about how much further along they are in their music careers—whether they've been signed to a label or been releasing music or gigging. Then I look at myself and think I'm a failure compared to these cool and talented people."

Our other daughter chimed in, "Well we're definitely related because I always think I'm the biggest one of my friends, and mom thinks everything is her fault." Then she turned to her brother and asked, "Oakley, what negative stuff do you think?"

He didn't skip a beat: "I'm not getting involved in this conversation, you guys are depressing." That made us all laugh, and then one of the girls turned back to Chris, "No seriously, Dad, how do you take those glasses off? Especially when I *do* think I'm a bad person? And I have all kinds of evidence to prove it."

My theme song (and boy am I sick of it!).

My kids were onto something with this conversation, because for the first 40 years of my life, my theme song was, "I've messed everything up."

For me, it sounds like, *I might as well just flush the last 40 years down the toilet, because I blew it in college and law school and in the first part of my marriage and was a terrible parent. If only I'd been more successful, and had the house where all the kids hung out, and had the money to join a country club, and been there for every birthday party, and every lacrosse game, bought Amazon stock ten years ago (Wait! There's more!!), lived on a different street, had a different friend group, made different choices.*

If only I did it right. And now, it's too late. It's all my fault.

Rebuilding your self-esteem
and self-respect one brick at a time.

You've got some version of that in your head too. You've made a million mistakes in your career, relationships, or with your health, and now it's too late. You screwed up your life, so you might as well flush it down the toilet. Right? Well, let me tell you, that was me.

As I write this sentence, it's even hard for me to believe how far I've come. You'll hear a part of the horror story shortly, but just a few years ago my life was a slow-motion train wreck. My confidence was in the gutter because I was dealing with bankruptcy, a failing marriage, crushing anxiety, and unemployment. I faced these issues like a lot of high-functioning adults do: by numbing myself with alcohol, screaming at my husband, and doing anything I could to avoid my problems.

I wish I were kidding. Honestly, it's why I have so much conviction about the tools and research I share. I've used everything I'm teaching you to save my own life. That's how I know they work.

After ten years of hard work, I've rewritten the story of my life. I'm now an entrepreneur, a best-selling author, and one of the most booked speakers in the world. If you watch my YouTube channel, you'll see the person I've become—someone who confidently goes after what she wants and crushes it in business. Someone who has nurtured an imperfectly beautiful 25-year marriage with three awesome kids. I am in the place I'm meant to be: I love myself, I feel comfortable in my own skin, and I work hard every single day on maintaining a rock-solid relationship with myself. And you're meant to be in this place, too.

I still don't live on the right street, or belong to that country club, and I can't redo my college and law school years, but I did break the habit of obsessing over my past and constantly bashing myself for it. There is no fast track to transformation. You have to work on it in little ways every day. You can't buy self-esteem or self-love. You have to build it. A club membership or a different house won't change what's inside you. It takes sweat equity. You have to stand face-to-face with that part of you that you hate, forgive yourself for the hurt you've caused (especially to yourself), and do the work to become a better you. It's the only way to create the self-respect and build the self-esteem that you desire.

You can change.

There ARE do-overs in life. You get one every single morning when you wake up, look in the mirror, and decide who you are going to be today. You can choose. You can change. You can't go back in time but you can have your own back as you use the time you have to take control, change your behavior, and create a new chapter that makes you proud.

The hardest part is flipping your focus from what you hate toward what you want to create. Remember: the windshield in a car is bigger than the rearview mirror for good reason. You're not supposed to go backward; you're supposed to drive forward and that means you must look AHEAD.

Yes, you've screwed up. Me too. The worst things that you've done, witnessed, or survived are your most powerful teachers. Stop making yourself wrong over what happened and unpack it. Understand it. Learn the lessons woven into every mistake you've made and every painful thing you've experienced.

I'll go first. Let's take a look at the gnarly, almost unrecognizable BEFORE picture of my life. I'm going to take you into two moments in my life that are cringe-worthy stories and sadly 100% true.

A terrible, horrible, no good, very bad three years.

One of the worst periods of my life was during law school, which is where my anxiety that had been building since childhood culminated in a wildly self-destructive streak. For three years straight, I woke up in a panic, because once I got to law school, I knew I didn't want to be a lawyer. But since I had no clue what I wanted to do with my life, I had no idea what else to do.

I was constantly on edge, stressed out, falling behind, and my thoughts, actions, and habits just perpetuated those feelings. Plus, I was surrounded by all of these people who were excited to be in law school, which made me feel like I didn't belong there. I felt incredibly alone. I hated all the reading and writing that are requirements for being a lawyer. I hadn't yet learned that I have dyslexia and ADHD. I was on a path of self-destruction.

My daily routine was as follows: Wake up hungover. Think, *Damn it, I'm late. Why do I keep doing this?* Stare at the ceiling thinking about my classes for the day and how behind I am on my homework. Light a cigarette as I race around the apartment. Drive to Dunkin' Donuts and order the biggest cup of coffee with cream and three sugars. Drive to class. Sit in class and panic about being called on. Pick at a salad for lunch. Sit alone in the library and try to study. Procrastinate for several hours talking to a friend. Drive home. Split a bottle of wine with my roommate and fall asleep. Wake up hungover.

It was the perfect routine for creating a big, fat, disappointing life for myself, right? And I didn't stop there. I kept going . . .

I repeated that pattern every day for three years, and even explaining it to you right now, I can try to laugh it off but honestly, it makes me sick to my stomach. I spent the whole time anxious and on edge. I barely remember anything. If you look at my patterns of thought and behavior, the choices I was making every day were keeping me locked in a painful and broken cycle. The negative thoughts (all variations on *You Mess Everything Up*) came at me in such a barrage that I could not focus on anything but surviving the day. The more I repeated this cycle, the more on edge I got. Negative thoughts fry your nervous system. *The negative thoughts and feelings create a downward spiral you don't know how to escape.*

When you're in survival mode, it usually gets worse until you hit bottom. And boy, did it get worse.

I really botched up my first year. Then I really screwed things up.

That first summer of law school, I interned at the attorney general's office in Grand Rapids, Michigan. The AG asked me to do a research project on recidivism rates in Michigan. It was an incredible opportunity. Not only would I have learned a great deal on a topic that mattered to me, but I also would have an incredible building block for my future—I was working directly for the attorney general of a state! But I was so overwhelmed by a project that size that I never even started. I didn't even crack open a book. Not one.

Here we go again . . .

My anxiety was so chronic that I don't remember driving to But I do remember this: the AG called me into his office near the end of the summer. My face was bright red and I was sweating profusely through my suit jacket. I made up a billion excuses for why the project was delayed. I walked out the door and never went back. I didn't even quit; I just disappeared. I guess I was ghosting people before it was a thing. Honestly, I'm so embarrassed that I've never written about this story before.

Another year, I landed an amazing summer job at a law firm in New Mexico, and a week before it was supposed to start, I had a massive panic attack over the thought of getting on a plane to fly across the country and living alone for the summer. I called the firm and lied, saying there had been a family emergency and I wasn't coming.

Does this sound like the Mel Robbins you know? As you observe my story, you can see that my negative thoughts (*I can't do this*) triggered negative feelings (*anxiety*) and negative actions (*run away*), and created a spiral. And once you start spiraling, it takes some kind of force to break that centrifugal spin. I'm going to emphasize negative thoughts—*I can't do this, I hate myself, I'm a wreck all the time*—because when you are so used to hearing them, you may not realize they are there. You also don't realize how these thoughts, when repeated, create a life of their own.

Of course, I wanted to be successful and strong. And of course, I wanted these opportunities. But my mind was so obsessed with the narrative I invested in (say it with me: *I. Mess. Everything. Up.*), I could not perceive the massive project with the AG or the summer job in New Mexico as opportunities. As soon as something felt overwhelming, I had to shoot them down or run for the hills— because that's what you do when you believe you screw everything up. Even if it means you leave your dreams by the roadside.

And naturally, once I bailed on these two wonderful opportunities, it only made me feel worse about myself. The downward spiral deepened. More negative thoughts. More shame too, which takes your spirit right down with it.

This is so foundationally important that I need to repeat it: when your negative thoughts increase, you may get trapped in the spin cycle of catastrophic thinking. That's basically what I did during law school: I piled on the negative thoughts until I suffocated. I hit rock bottom. I felt like a gigantic sledgehammer smashed my life into pieces. And I was the one wielding it. No matter what I did to try to fix it, I constantly crashed and burned.

I had none of the tools you are about to learn. I didn't know the link between my childhood trauma and my self-destructive behavior. I also didn't know how to stop aiming my mistakes at myself. I didn't know how to stop believing that the bad things proved that I was intrinsically a bad person. I was so ashamed of myself and things I kept doing. So I did what most people in pain or crisis do—I tried to numb it. There are a million ways we numb ourselves and try to bury pain: alcohol, drugs, impulsive shopping, emotional eating.

Are you counting? Because it's about to get even worse.

I did all of those things to numb, and I also started cheating on my law school boyfriend with my ex from college, because psychologists will tell you—sex in secrecy is an intoxicating stress reliever . . . but I will tell you it's also a powder keg of destruction that implodes your life. That's what happened to me, because eventually, they both found out. *Another colossal fail, Mel.* And it's not lost on me how significant it is that I was screwing up my life by cheating on my boyfriend, and even THAT I messed up because they both found out . . . I was screwing up my screwup?! That is some grade A dysfunction going on. I am not proud to admit the things I did while I was just trying to survive. I am telling you this story to prove to you that if you are trapped in a shame cycle or loop of self-destructive behavior, there is a way out. If I can change, so can you.

This is not my comeback story.

Luckily, my big crash and burn led me to the place where my lifelong personal growth journey began: the therapist's couch.

It was there that I began to understand that I was doing this to myself. Not intentionally, of course, but that I had childhood trauma and patterns of thinking, belief, and behavior that had become the default in my subconscious mind and kept taking me down these crazy self-sabotaging paths.

With the guidance of my therapist, I was finally able to face what had happened to me and all the horrible things that I'd done to try to survive. She also helped me see that I had to take responsibility for all the crap happening in my life from here on out. I was honest about how I led myself *way* down this road that felt so far from home—far from who I really was. And still, I hated myself for hitting rock bottom. (Another mess to add to the list, Mel!) *How did I let it get so bad?* Like our daughter, my belief was "I'm a bad person" and my life seemed to prove it. I continued to trash-talk myself. I knew those negative thoughts were bringing me down, but I had no idea how to silence the relentless beatdown in my head.

This was decades before podcasts, online courses, or a variety of self-help books were available. This is why I'm so passionate about this topic and unapologetic in sharing my struggles because so many times I have felt alone and lost.

This is your comeback story.

But here's the profound insight I gained that I want you to hear: *When you think you've messed something up, you start to hate yourself. When you hate yourself, you inevitably do things you hate.* Your thoughts create a downward spiral.

I've also learned the opposite is true: When you love yourself, you inevitably do things you love. When you treat yourself with respect, you do respectable things. And when you celebrate yourself, you do things worth celebrating. As we talked about earlier, you can change this—right now, it's your subconscious and all your past programming vs. YOU.

Interrupting those self-loathing feelings that take you so low—shame, regret, failure, zero self-worth—forces you to see the truth. You aren't broken, you're blocked. You may have done some things that are pretty bad, but YOU are not a bad person. You didn't know how to act differently because you didn't understand what a critical role your constant negative thoughts, past trauma, and upbringing have on you. The first step: FORGIVE YOURSELF for all the things you did while you were just trying to survive. The next step: SILENCE, then EVICT that bully that lives in your head.

CHAPTER 6

Where's All This Negative Crap Coming From?

Everyone has a negative mantra or belief about themselves: *I screw everything up. I'm a bad person. I'm ugly. I'm a failure. Blah. Blah. Blah.*

Maybe you have failed and screwed things up royally. Maybe you aren't winning beauty pageants. Maybe you are the shortest one of all your friends. All that may be true. But:

Is thinking these things helping you? Isn't it time to feel better about yourself?

My husband is right—you've got to be careful to not let this negative story get stuck on replay in your head. The question is, how the heck do you remove it? Especially if you do look in the mirror and have a lot of regrets, doubts, and disappointment. Believe it or not, the steps are as straightforward as doing a load of laundry.

My laundry and your negative thoughts.

I can't tell you how many times I've opened up the dryer to put in a load and *AGAIN!* the lint screen is clogged. *Am I the only one in this house who knows how to take my forefinger and thumb to peel the lint off the screen, people?* There is always a thick, padded layer of fuzz that completely clogs the screen. One day, as I was cleaning the dryer filter, I had an epiphany. Just like that dryer filter, you and I have all kinds of crap inside of us that has built up over time.

Those inescapable negative thoughts? They're like fuzzy residue from your life. The residue has been accumulating since you were a kid in the form of: other people's opinions, negative self-talk, rejections, disappointments, heartbreak, discrimination, trauma, guilt, and self-doubt. These experiences have created *mental lint.* It clogs your mind and blocks you from being able to celebrate YOU.

There's a lot more to this than a cute metaphor. In your brain, there is a filter. It's called the Reticular Activating System, or RAS, for short. I call it a *filter,* because negative experiences tend to get stuck in the RAS, but technically it is a live network of neurons that sits like a hairnet over your brain. When your RAS is jammed with thoughts, beliefs, and experiences from your past, you stay stuck in the past. That's why you keep repeating the same mistakes, thinking the same negative thoughts, and living in the echo chamber of your mind.

The High 5 Habit and all the tools in this book are like taking your thumb and forefinger to the lint in the filter and peeling off all that crap that's built up. That's also why I want you to practice it every day. You can't do a load of laundry without creating lint, and you can't live a day in your life without feeling or thinking something that makes you feel like crap. The key is to not let that negative stuff build up. You need to learn how to clear that residue out of your system every day so it doesn't stick.

Say hello to your new best friend, RAS.

Some experts call the RAS *the bouncer for your mind* or *the gatekeeper.* Your RAS has a huge job: it decides (filters) what information gets into your conscious mind and what information stays out. Every day, your RAS must police 34 gigabytes of data.

(That's three years' worth of phone data in 24 hours!) I want you to embrace what an enormous job your RAS has and why it needs your help so it can help you. Honestly, it needs more than your help—it needs a hug, because it's been working overtime, and it's been filtering the world through all your old crap.

Your RAS blocks 99% of what's around you from reaching your conscious mind—because if it didn't, your head would explode from information overload. There are only four things that always get past your RAS and into your conscious mind:

- The sound of your name being called

- Anything that threatens your safety or the safety of your loved ones

- Signals that your partner is interested in having sex.

- Whatever your RAS thinks is important to you (and that means whatever thought you repeat or topic you focus on, your RAS will think is important)

This last point is EVERYTHING because if you know what's important to you, you can train your RAS to filter the world every day and help you find it. Let the power of that sink in for a moment. You can teach your mind to find things you WANT to see, things that elevate and support you, that make you feel happier and proud, things that lead you to your dreams. Right now, your RAS believes you want to see the same world you saw in middle school, because you haven't changed your opinion of yourself since then!

It's time to clean your filter.

When you know how to use it, your RAS becomes a searchlight, sweeping the path ahead of you and shining its beam on all the opportunities and synchronicities and hidden surprises that are waiting for you, just around the next corner. When you tell your RAS what to see, it works FOR you. But here's the catch. If your negative thoughts—*I'm a failure, I'm a bad person, I'm not good enough, Nothing works out for me so why try*—are the soundtrack of your life, your RAS will search for every block, every obstacle, every pitfall to prove your storyline.

Take my husband, Chris, who for a long time believed *I am a failure* and for years that's all he could see when he looked in the mirror. He had all kinds of "evidence" to back it up. He jumped from job to job early in his career, then he opened a pizza restaurant and wholesale business. Friends and family invested, he and his best friend poured their hearts and souls into it, and after seven years, it closed its doors.

Those last few years, as the business was failing, were a horrible rollercoaster ride to go through. There were liens on the house and the crushing debt and fear were inescapable, unless we were too drunk to think about them. Which we often were. When Chris left the business, he was destroyed. A shell of himself. I became the breadwinner because we had no other option (something I was pissed off about at the time) and by the grace of God (and a tremendous amount of work), I realize now, this is exactly what I was meant to do. I would never want to relive those years—the anxiety was so crushing at times I could barely get out of bed.

I didn't want to be responsible for my own life, my own healing, and my future. I was so angry when I realized that Chris wasn't going to rescue me. As much as I hated it, I knew the truth: If this crushing situation was going to turn around, it had to start with me. *You have to fight,* I told myself. *You have to find a reason to get out of bed. Even if that reason is just so that you don't waste an hour drowning in fear. You must anchor down on a goal to push yourself toward it, even if the goal is just to wake up and not feel so horrible today.*

The decision that changed my life at that moment was simply to get my ass out of bed. I decided to launch myself through the fear instead of lying there marinating in fear. When you are at an emotional rock bottom, you must find the courage to say *I'm not doing this to myself—I'm changing.* That's when I invented "The 5 Second Rule." Just like NASA uses a 5-4-3-2-1 countdown to launch a rocket, I counted down 5-4-3-2-1 to launch myself into action before my negative thoughts pinned me down. I'm dead serious. Alarm rings. No staring at the ceiling. No panic attack. No snooze button. No rolling over and shoving your head under the pillow to blot out the day. 5-4-3-2-1: kick your own ass.

I used the Rule to launch myself out of bed. I used it to stop pointing my anger at Chris for where we were and start directing my fire and energy toward fixing what I could. I used it to stop drinking so much. I used it to make cold calls that led to a part-time job at a digital marketing agency, and to land a radio audition and start hosting a Saturday morning advice show. I used it to reach out to friends. To tell the truth. To ask for help. To get up every day and do it again. And again. And again. Slowly, day by day, my life started to change, because I was changing how I lived my day-to-day life. And just like running that marathon, you change your life one step at a time. Boy, I wish I had also known about the High 5 Habit at this moment in time, because the voice in my head would not shut up. This all would have been so much easier to handle if I had been kinder and more encouraging of myself along the way.

A new path forward . . .

I am grateful for the 5 Second Rule and all the lessons I learned. I look back on hitting rock bottom and clawing our way out with a completely different view than Chris. Without that painful period in our lives, there would be no success story. There would be no 5 Second Rule. I am grateful for what that taught me about my own strength and the power of forgiveness. I am grateful that Chris became a stay-at-home parent to our three kids for a few years while working on his own need to heal. He had always wanted to be around more when the kids got older, and as my speaking business grew, Chris stepped in and played a critical role in helping build it.

My view of this chapter of our lives was that the business failure led us to a wonderful new situation and the right roles in our marriage, in life, and within our family. I thought this painful experience paved the road to an incredible success story, and honestly, I thought it was behind us.

. . . But that's not how Chris viewed it AT ALL.

Everywhere he looked he saw evidence that he was a complete failure. If he was picking up the kids from school, it meant he was a failure. If he was mowing the lawn at home, it meant he was a failure. If he was cooking dinner, he was a failure. Serving as the president of the high school Boosters, he was a failure. The fact that our kids say the time they got to spend with him during those years was one of the greatest gifts of their childhood, doesn't change how Chris felt about himself. He was a failure.

And when he started working again, his story stayed the same. He was the CFO of "Mel's" business, a reminder that he had failed at his business. It didn't matter how much it is "our" business, or that on paper he legally was a 50% co-owner of our business. He just couldn't shake the unworthiness and shame he felt for failing at "his" career and "losing" other people's money in the restaurant venture.

We all do this to ourselves.

This is the soundtrack of everyday life, just switch out Chris's belief (I'm a failure) with your own (I screw everything up, Everyone hates me, and on and on and on). Chris's story (and countless ones of my own) are just examples of how your RAS can take your entire life off the rails. I'm sure you can see a similar pattern in your own life. As you start to repeat your core negative belief, that bouncer in your mind, the RAS, filters the world to confirm those beliefs. When Chris was standing on the lacrosse field coaching our daughter's lacrosse team, he didn't see it as a huge success to have this kind of flexibility and time. He focused on the one dad pacing back and forth along the sidelines on his cell phone—probably on a conference call for work, and *boom*—it confirmed Chris's belief. *I'm a failure. I shouldn't be coaching, that should be me.*

If I told him that he was the best dad in the world, and that I could not do what I was doing without HIM, I was wasting my breath—the bouncer in his mind blocked it because it didn't match his belief. If he was meeting with our accountant and doing tax planning for next year, it wasn't our business he was the CFO of, it was mine. Again, he had failed.

The important thing to take away from all this is that, just like a computer, your brain has specific programming. No one else can change it. Just like I can't change my husband's or my daughter's beliefs, I can't change yours either. YOU have to decide that you're tired of thinking this crap. The programming (your beliefs and your RAS) is something you can CHANGE. Your mind is standing by, just waiting for you to tell it how to help you, and your RAS is the key.

And perhaps this will help you too: No one else is still thinking about what happened five years ago, but you. No one else is keeping score as diligently as you. You are the one cataloging all your flaws, mistakes, and problems, and it's keeping you focused on (you guessed it!) all your flaws, mistakes, and problems. It's creating these toxic, untrue beliefs about yourself that act like walls, keeping you trapped in the past. How about you let yourself out of that mental jail? You've served your time. You've beaten yourself up. It's time to free yourself from the past and start focusing on the future you want to create. It starts with recognizing that you do have a story or belief about yourself. And that belief is bringing you down.

Chris started doing the work inside himself to heal—meditation, therapy, he became a practicing Buddhist, he started making amends. After several years, he found his own path toward greater meaning in his life. He started a retreat for men called Soul Degree; a chance for men to get together to do what men never do: take time for themselves to connect with other men about their life experiences and reconnect to something deeper within themselves and the greater forces in life. If Chris and I can turn our lives around, so can you, using your RAS.

You're the boss of your RAS.

I'm sure you've had the experience of being broken up with, and for days, weeks, or even months, all you can do is see things that remind you of your ex. You listen to sad songs on repeat. You mope around. You stalk them online. All of which tells your RAS that your ex is still important. Even though you haven't seen them in weeks or months, reminders are everywhere.

Then, suddenly, you meet somebody new, and it's like the bouncer in your mind kicked your ex out of the line and let your new lover move to the front. Next thing you know, all you see are people in love, all you hear are love songs, and it seems like everyone in the world is just as happy as you. Your RAS did that. And you know what you don't see anymore? Signs of your ex.

When what's important to you changes, the way you see the world and yourself changes too. Your RAS filters out all the old shit and crappy feelings related to your ex and opens the door for things related to your new love. It will do the exact same thing for you when you decide that it's time to stop beating yourself up.

The stories you tell yourself (about yourself) are so crucial. If you keep repeating the story that *you're a failure or a bad person*, or picking apart your appearance, or your bank account, your RAS will believe it's important and only show you more reasons to believe that you are a failure or a bad person.

The flip side of that is true too. If you change the story you tell yourself from *I'm a bad person* to *I'm a work in progress and I keep getting better*, the more you repeat it, the faster that bouncer in your brain will respond.

Flip It.

I'm going to give you a different way to look at life. If you are willing to try it, along with the High 5 Challenge, you will see real and exciting changes in your life. Let's get started.

> **Current Limiting Belief:** *I screw everything up. I am a failure.*
>
> **Flip It:** *I FORGIVE myself for the things I did when I was trying to survive. Every day I am becoming a better version of myself.*

Here's the truth: When you believe you make everything in your life a disaster, you are simply believing in the wrong thing. By saying, "I ruin everything" you attest to two things: (1) you are so powerful that you consistently create only one type of outcome in your life, with no variations, and (2) that outcome is bad. Think about that for a second: You are so influential, so omnipresent, such a force of nature that when you get near something, even something good, it changes into disaster. I have to tell you this is a VERY good place to start. Stay with me.

A truth and a lie.

You are on to one truth: you ARE powerful. But you already know that. You see evidence of your power everywhere; it's in all the messes you've made in your life. You would not be able to create such a consistent track record of colossal crap in your life if you were powerless. Can you see that?

Looking back, I can count all the problems I created in my life: in law school, my two jobs, my two boyfriends. And hitting rock bottom in my 40s and blaming Chris. There were piles of crap EVERYWHERE and I managed to step in each and every one. I want you to look at all the messes you've made. If you can create such a heaping pile of stinking poop in your life, here's the other truth: *you also have the power to create something really amazing.*

If you can create all those piles of garbage, why can't you create piles of glitter instead?

Amazing outcomes can materialize just as easily as bad ones. I'm serious. But it all has to do with what you BELIEVE you are capable of and what you are focused on. If you are focused on how you create bad things in your life, you have to flip it. Flip that belief on its head.

Take action: If you get up in the morning and look in the mirror with an *Ugh* reaction, you get a life of *Ugh*.

Start your day with a high five in the mirror and "I forgive myself and I am becoming a better version of myself" and there is a new world outside your door. "I don't like this, but I can control how I respond."

Right now, you have the great skill and habit of looking at things in a certain way. What if you built the same kind of strong skill set but went for the OPPOSITE result.

What if you swiped left instead of right?

Instead of saying, "Again! I dropped the ball." Say, "How can I fix this?" "How can I make this situation the best outcome for me? What is in my control?" *I screwed it up* is not your only option for an outcome. Think about that.

One last thing: If you are going to take all the credit for messing things up, at least take the credit for when things go right. Here are some other statements to help you flip the belief:

I can solve any problem. (*I can clean up any mess.*)

This is preparing me for something amazing that's coming. (*If it's preparing me, I'm not messing up, I'm learning.*)

You were born with it.

And here's another cool thing about your RAS—training it to work for you is going to be so easy. This mental flexibility is already inside you. You've already experienced the power of your RAS and didn't even realize it. Isn't that great? Let me show you what I mean and how willing your RAS is to help you! I have an example to illustrate the power of your RAS: shopping for a new car.

Let's say you're in the market for a new car and you've decided to test-drive a red Acura. You like it because (1) red is a fabulous color, and (2) you don't know anybody who drives an Acura. Plus, you read that it's a reliable and safe car.

Now, as you're reading this book, I want you to stop and think: When's the last time you remember seeing a red Acura? Unless you own one or work in an Acura dealership, I bet you can't think of when that was because until this moment, it wasn't important to you. And since it wasn't important to you, your RAS was blocking all red Acuras out of your conscious mind.

Those red Acuras are out there, driving right past you every day, but they weren't IMPORTANT to you until now. Your brain can't consciously process every single make and model of every single car that is driving past you or parked on the side of the road. This is part of the information overload that your RAS is constantly blocking from your conscious mind. Of course, you "see" all those cars. You're just not registering any information. They come and they go. They pass through the filter in your brain. Just like our daughter "sees" all the people at the bar who aren't as perfect as she imagines, but they are just not registering.

But the second you start thinking about buying a red Acura, your RAS is so nimble that it will change its own filtering system on a dime. Thinking about the purchase of a red Acura has lit up that spaghetti strainer on your head. This network of neurons only gets stronger when you read about it, when you test-drive it, when you comparison shop, when you sign the paperwork, when you drive it off the lot, and when you post about it on Instagram. All these thoughts and actions tell your RAS that YOU love red Acuras. Suddenly, overnight, you won't be able to drive down the road without seeing red Acuras. That's because the bouncer in your mind just pulled the red Acura from the subconscious part of your brain all the way to the front of your subconscious mind.

This is just one of a million examples of how your RAS is trying so damn hard to show you what it thinks is important to YOU. It only blocks out all the times your daughter turns to you and says *I feel so lucky that you are home, Dad* and locks in on the businessman on the cell phone because your RAS thinks YOU want to feel like a failure. You've felt like a failure in your career for so long that your RAS thinks it is important to you. And the same is true if you think: *I'm a bad person.* If you think you are a bad person, you'll feel like one after every difficult conversation. You'll focus on your friend's reaction and ignore the fact that you should be proud of yourself for drawing a boundary.

Here's the escape hatch.

Let me unpack this even further because this is so critical. When you repeat negative self-talk, your RAS believes it's important. Just like the red Acura, your RAS is scanning your environment for ways to affirm negative thoughts like: "I look disgusting," "I hate my body," "Why can't I be pretty?" Your thoughts tell your RAS what's important. That's why you feel trapped in a world that feels aimed against you.

Retraining your RAS to get out of the self-degradation begins in the bathroom mirror every single morning. What you say to that person in the mirror and how you treat them matters. So starting tomorrow, you better wake up every day and high five yourself, because your RAS is watching. It always is.

I am explaining this in excruciating detail because I need you to understand why this high five thing is going to work. I know you're skeptical—that's the reason why I am explaining all the science, and unpacking how your past experiences have impacted your beliefs, and how the filter in your brain works and why it needs your help. That bouncer in your brain wants to HELP you.

Right now you have a tendency to live in a low mental and emotional state—thanks to your past. That's why you have low confidence, low self-esteem, and low levels of motivation. The High 5 Habit flips this on its head and helps you restore yourself back to the higher mental and emotional state that you were designed for—a state that inspires you to take action. I've said it before and I'll say it again. You cannot think your way to a new life. You must act your way there, one high five at a time. Taking consistent action toward change is not always easy, but you can do it.

Change the way you look at the world, and the world you're looking at changes.

Yes, it is that simple. And let me repeat—I understand that your problems are big and overwhelming and real. The High 5 Habit doesn't change those realities. It changes YOU. How you see yourself and what you are capable of achieving. How YOU see the world and what opportunities or solutions you can create. And it's how YOU push yourself forward grounded in faith and belief that when you do, something amazing will happen.

Every single day, your brain will start to get the new message about what's important to YOU and to your future. It will fall in line and begin to filter the world in an entirely new way to help you get what you want. Seeing things differently won't make your problems disappear, but it will have you seeing different solutions, different opportunities, and different possibilities that you haven't seen before. And that makes all the difference in the world.

The question is, aside from that high five, how else can I train my RAS to work for me? Brace yourself, this is going to sound just as silly as high fiving yourself in the mirror. At least, that was our daughter's reaction. So let's get those dark glasses off, chuck those horrible things you say in the trash, and start training your brain to see you and your future in a whole new way.

CHAPTER 7

Why Am I Suddenly Seeing Hearts Everywhere?

As I explained the High 5 Habit to our daughters, one of them said, "So if I high five myself in the mirror, I'll stop thinking I'm a bad person? *Really?*"

Knowing how skeptical she sounded, I decided to take a different approach.

"I know this sounds unbelievable, but what if I could prove that you can change your opinion of yourself in real time?"

"If I could actually stop thinking *I'm a bad person* all the time?" she said. "That'd be cool."

I explained the red Acura example to them and a light bulb went off: "Oh yeah. I've experienced that. My roommate got a VW Bug. I'd never even been in one before. Now I see them everywhere! It's crazy."

I said, "Exactly. That's your brain changing the way you see the world—in real time. Right now, you say '*I'm a bad person*' and you probably see things every day that make you think it's true. Correct?"

She said, "Yes. Like the fact that I missed my dentist appointment yesterday. I forgot and immediately told myself, '*There I go again screwing everything up.*'"

"That's a great example. Now, let's flip it. Let's teach your mind to NOT see all the stuff happening in your life as evidence that you are bad. You can forget a dentist's appointment and just let it pass through your mind without attaching '*I'm a bad person.*' You just have to be deliberate and tell your mind exactly what you want to think about yourself, when things mess up."

She looked really curious. "Really? How?"

"First, let's train your mind by playing a simple game that changes the way you see the world in real time. Every day, look for naturally occurring heart shapes in the world around you. Whether it's a heart-shaped rock, or a heart-shaped leaf, or a heart-shaped oil stain on the floor of your garage, or a heart-shaped swirl of milk on the top of your cappuccino—anything counts."

"You mean the same way you are always looking for heart-shaped rocks when we are walking on the beach?"

"Yes."

"Seriously? That is the stupidest thing I've ever heard, Mom."

Our other daughter chimed in: "I agree. How does that help me stop feeling like the biggest one of my friends? Especially when I am? I want you to teach me how to be happy and to be successful and make a lot of money in my new career. You're a self-help person. How do rocks on the ground help me change my opinion of myself?"

Don't worry. I had a great answer. I told them, "The point of this exercise is to train your mind to spot things you currently block out and prove to yourself that you can make your brain work for you by telling it what is important to YOU. And if you want to make a lot of money, you'd better train your mind to see the opportunities and deals that other people walk right by, just like the 'stupid heart rock on the ground' that you miss because you aren't looking for it. And if you want to stop thinking you're bad or hating the way you look, you better train your mind to stop attaching that thought to everything you see."

I could tell they were considering my argument. So, I went further, "Besides, if I told either one of you to repeat a positive mantra *'I am beautiful'*, or *'I'm a good person'*, you would think, *This is stupid*, because you don't believe it right now. So first I've got to show the power you have to change what your mind sees. Then you'll trust what I'm saying and use these 'stupid' tools to change how you see yourself."

Good people mess up all the time. It doesn't make you a bad person. And even if you are, why does that make you unlovable? It's all about flipping the way you look at things so you feel empowered and supported. And imagine how much easier and even fulfilling it would be if you could silence the beatdown and love yourself as you work on your health goals. Now that I had them convinced, they wanted to know how to do the heart exercise.

It's your turn. I'm serious.

Starting tomorrow, find one naturally occurring heart shape in the world around you. When you find it, stop, and look at it. Take a photo of it. Savor the moment for a minute. I see one every day and I still think it's pretty cool every time it happens. Looking for hearts will turn your life into a scavenger hunt where you wake up every day knowing at some point today, you'll stumble across that little secret heart you're meant to find.

Not only does this exercise wake you up to the power of your RAS and how quickly your mind changes when you tell it what you want to see, it proves to you that there's a different way to see the world around you. And that means there's a different way to see yourself and your place in it.

If you try this and you don't see a heart, it's probably because you're skeptical or you think it's stupid, so you've told the RAS,

"This isn't important." If you want to have an open mind, and flip these negative thoughts, you have to remove what is preventing you from taking action in your life. Skepticism, doubt, and cynicism are like lint in a dryer. They block you. This is a way to practice optimism and positive mindset changes in a low-stakes, simple situation. Besides, if you can't play an easy game with heart rocks, you won't be able to play the game of spotting opportunity when the stakes are higher.

See the world differently.

Do this exercise for a week, and you'll realize there's an entire world that you walk by every day that your mind is currently not allowing you to experience. I've been doing this for years, and I continue to find a heart every single day. If you follow me on social media, you'll see that I post the hearts I find all the time, and every day people around the world tag me and share the hearts that they are finding.

And here's how you can amplify it even more: Assume that each heart was intentionally planted there for you to find. When you do find one, close your eyes for a moment, smile, and see if you can feel that warm wave of connection to a larger force, one that you can't quite explain. This is what I do and it makes me feel like God and the universe have my back and are guiding me.

There are forces at work that are trying to help you to see the world differently. There are clues that will lead you to the goals and accomplishments that have eluded you. You've just been looking at things the wrong way. Once you've started finding those hearts, you'll be amazed that your mind does in fact change to see what you tell it to see.

Why Am I Suddenly Seeing Hearts Everywhere?

When you get really good at this, you'll be able to make some crazy stuff appear in your life. I'm sure you've had the experience of looking back on your life and seeing how the dots connect, leading you to where you are now. What's cool about training your RAS to see what YOU want to see, is that it helps you start connecting the dots forward, from this moment to the future you envision. Your mind is designed to help you get what you want when you use the tools in this book. In Chapter 14, I will tell you an unbelievable story and unpack the science of how I used my RAS and an unwavering belief to manifest something miraculous into my life—and how you can too.

Creating new beliefs.

Now that you know about the RAS and have started looking for hearts, it's time to work on those negative beliefs that run on repeat in your head. It's time to clear it away by interrupting the old thought patterns and replacing them with how you *want* to feel.

There are three steps to changing the soundtrack in your head that I want you to start implementing:

Step one: "I'm not thinking about that."

Negative thoughts will always pop up. You can't stop that from happening, but you CAN interrupt them. Here's how: use a verbal High 5 Habit to swat that negative thought away. You can choose what you think about. That means you can also choose what you don't think about. As soon as that negative thought crosses your mind—*Nothing works out, I always screw up, No one will ever love me*—interrupt it with five powerful words that redirect your RAS: **"I'm not thinking about that."**

That's what it means to check the filter—you check in with your thoughts. It's dead simple, but if you are an overthinker, a worrier, a catastrophizer, paralyzed by fears, or struggling with anxiety, this is life changing. In a moment, I'll tell you how to properly retrain your RAS to default to what you WANT to think, but allow me to linger here for a minute and truly explain what I am asking you to do. This part—interrupt the worry and wipe it away like lint on a dryer filter—is critical.

When I started doing this a few years ago, I was trying to interrupt the thoughts that made me feel anxious. It was shocking how many times per day I had to say "I'm not thinking about that." That in itself was eye-opening: just how frequently my negative soundtrack was playing tunes in my mind.

If a friend didn't respond to an email or phone call right away, the negative voice would say, *They must be mad at me*. But then I'd catch myself and say, "I'm not thinking about that."

If I saw someone online posting a photo of their feet on a lounge chair with the ocean in the background, I'd feel jealous and I'd hear the voice say, *Hate. Her.* and then immediately I'd bash myself: *I'll never afford that kind of vacation*, until I stopped it with "I'm not thinking about that."

If I saw myself wearing shorts in a photo, I'd automatically start to tear myself down: *God, my cellulite is gross*, until: "I'm not thinking about that."

Your negative voice has one weakness: it hates being interrupted and told to shut up. One at a time, you can slap those negative thoughts away before they get stuck in your mind. Remember: from the very beginning of this book, I have told you that your mind is designed to help you get what you want. You came into this world a little risk-taking explorer and a fearless trier of new things. You believed in yourself and loved seeing yourself in a mirror. These tools you're learning tap back into the essence of who you are.

Step two: Note to self.

Once you've talked back with "I'm not thinking about that," it's time to create a new belief that tells your RAS what you want it to see—*and then make it visual.* You've probably noticed that a lot of gyms and yoga or spin studios have motivational quotes on their walls: *Anything is possible. Inhale confidence, exhale doubt. Strength is in you. You got this.* This is an example of a visual cue placed right where you are taking action to change. I want you to do the same thing with the new meaningful mantra you are about to pick so that you are reminded of it and remember to use it.

Researchers from Harvard and Wharton found that people are more likely to follow through on good intentions when they set up a cue for themselves that is two things: (1) slightly unexpected (so it stands out to your brain), and (2) is in the exact place where you will do this habit. I recommend putting a cue on your bathroom mirror. That way, you'll be reminded to high five yourself and of your mantra each morning.

And what exactly should that new mantra be? I've already explained why most positive mantras don't work: your mind rejects them because you don't believe them. That's why you can't just start repeating "I'm a great person" or "I'm so beautiful" and expect your mind to show you evidence of it. It's crucial your meaningful mantra be one you can *believe right now.* So how do you do that? I'll give you a few that I love, but try a bunch and see what feels right to you.

Say it out loud and see how your mind responds. Do you come up with a million reasons why this new mantra isn't true? Then try another, until you've got one that your mind high fives back. You'll know it's meaningful because it will feel like you want to high five the mirror when you say it. It will immediately say YES! energetically inside of you. You'll know it when you find one that works for you.

Meaningful Mantras

I deserve to feel good today.
I am an awesome person.
I have my own back.
What broke my heart opened my eyes.
This is teaching me something I need to know.
Today is going to be a good day.
I am enough just as I am.
I will figure this out.
Every day, I'm getting a little stronger.
Don't believe me? Watch.
I can handle this. Bring it on.
What's meant for me is trying to find me.
I am stronger than I think.
I am allowed to be a work in progress.
This scares me and I'm doing it anyway.
My new chapter is just beginning.
The world needs my story.
I am growing every day.
I choose to focus on what I can control.
This moment is temporary.
If I put in the work, it will happen.

Since launching High5Challenge.com, I've heard from thousands of you about the little cues you've set up in your bathroom to remember this daily habit, and I want to share a few of my favorites:

- On a Post-it note, write out your mantra, and stick it on your mirror as a reminder to high five yourself.

- Trace your hand with lipstick or eyeliner on your bathroom mirror, and write your mantra below it.

- Trace your hand on construction paper, cut it out, write your mantra in the middle, and tape it to your mirror.

- Draw on your mirrors with a dry-erase marker.

- Fill a jar with messages to yourself. Each morning, high five yourself and pull one out!

- Put an object (the more random, the better) in your bathroom, and attach a note to it with your mantra.

Step three: Act like the person you want to become.

Now that you're talking back to your negative belief and saying your new mantra, comes the most crucial step: *You must take physical actions that match the new positive belief.*

One of the most effective ways to change your opinion of yourself is to tap into a body of research called Behavioral Activation Therapy. It's a simple but profoundly effective therapeutic method that asserts: *Act like the person you want to become, no matter how you feel right now.* In addition to creating momentum, this is powerful because your brain sees you taking action. Your old negative thoughts are so ingrained that you can't just talk your way out of your old habits and beliefs. You have to SEE yourself taking action to change.

The action *proves* that your new belief is true—and this helps your RAS change your filter even more quickly. And even better, when you treat yourself like you're worthy and lovable, you don't just shift your RAS—you also build self-acceptance, which as you learned earlier, is the most important mindset for happiness and satisfaction.

Let me give you some examples. If, like my daughter, you want to become a musician, but you're wracked with self-doubt, start acting like a person who puts themselves out there. That means write songs and post them online. Sign up to play a local gig. No matter how nervous, afraid, and doubting you are, do it anyway. When your mind sees you taking action, your RAS realizes this is important to you, and it opens up a world of options for you to be playing more music.

The same goes for self-love. If you're critical of your appearance, start acting like someone who loves themselves. Instead of poking and prodding yourself in the mirror, focus on what you appreciate. Make healthier choices because you deserve to feel good. Move your body not to fix yourself, but because you love yourself and deserve to feel good. Put those Post-its on your mirror. Compliment yourself. And make sure to high five yourself every morning to prove to your brain, "I'm the kind of person who celebrates myself just for being me."

And, to take it even deeper, and make this shift even faster, take action that helps another person. Get the focus off yourself. Call someone and ask them how they are doing. Go volunteer. When you're of service to others, in addition to just feeling really good, it snaps you out of your misery and makes you see yourself in a new light.

Putting it all together.

So, the next time you have a negative thought, interrupt it with "I'm not thinking about that." State your new belief. And then take an action that proves your belief is true, whether that's high fiving yourself in the mirror, or another action that proves to your brain: *It's important to me to feel this way.* This is how to change the story you tell yourself as well as the way your mind filters the world and what it sees in real time.

This is exactly what Kristien does. She started high fiving herself every day and found it shockingly powerful. After struggling with her weight and confidence, she found no exercise plan worked until she started to love herself. So, she became a certified health and fitness coach in Belgium, and started offering a program in which she teaches women exactly what worked for her: that physical health is grounded in how healthy your head is, and not about being a certain size. Health is about loving and taking care of yourself.

Kristien started teaching her clients to high five themselves in the mirror. She said, "When I first taught the high five, the women were shy about doing it—because they don't think they deserve it and that it's not normal to be number one for yourself. But as I see a woman giving herself a high five, and watch her grow more confident—that happiness and the smile it creates . . . no money in the world can match that!"

Then Kristien decided to take things up a notch. She started by putting up her new beliefs, including "You're improving every day" and "I'm proud of you" in her bathroom, so that she could repeat them as she high fived herself. After seeing how they were helping her, she added the beliefs to the mirror right in her entry-way, because she runs her coaching business out of her home. She wanted to make sure everyone who walked in saw them!

Isn't that amazing? She's found, once you're high fiving your-self and repeating your belief, it's easier to take action that proves you love yourself. She said, "One of the most important things to learn is to put yourself first. The high five and beliefs help you then act that way, as well."

Rewiring your mind.

Phew, we have covered A. LOT. High five to you and me. Well done! Let me recap quickly where we've been:

1. *Never leave a bathroom without high fiving yourself in the mirror.*

It creates new neural pathways in your brain to help make cheering for yourself your new default. Yes, life has left residue that is impacting the filter in your mind—but you can change that by adopting this new habit.

2. *Sign up for the #High5Challenge at High5Challenge.com.*

Let me support you! I'll provide the encouragement and accountability you need to complete this five-day challenge. It's free, and fun, so come join me!

3. *Identify your negative beliefs and experiment with flipping them.*

Talk back to those thoughts, replace them with a meaningful mantra you believe, and prove to your RAS—with physical action—that you want your mind to show you a new world filled with opportunities and positive things.

This is just the beginning.

Everything you are learning is helping you break patterns of thinking and behavior that keep you stuck. Back in Chapter 1, I explained that a high five symbolizes confidence, courage, and action. It's way more than a thing you do in the mirror—it's a holistic attitude about life. It's about cultivating and building an attitude and mindset in life that empowers you to take control, feel happier, and make meaningful changes. These tools will also help you clear away the lint from your past and create new positive beliefs about yourself and your future.

Now, I want to talk to you about the reality of life. There will be moments that sink your high five attitude, make you feel stuck and pessimistic, and strip away your confidence. You can always tell when that high five attitude has disappeared because you will not feel like taking action. I want to teach you how to flip these natural but negative emotional triggers. Once you understand them, you can move past them as simply as you can raise your hand and high five yourself in the mirror.

You have what you need to start changing your life, but I want to go even deeper and tackle the things that always trigger me emotionally and take me mentally low:

- *Jealousy*
- *Guilt*
- *Insecurity*

- *Unexpected setbacks*
- *Anxiety*
- *Fear*

Step-by-step, in the coming pages, you'll unpack these feelings and learn simple, proven strategies to get your high five mindset back and begin moving forward. At the end of the book, you'll also get a very simple guide for how you can implement everything you've learned about the High 5 Habit and cultivating a high five attitude in your daily life.

So, to begin, let's take a look at something that really gets me tied up in knots mentally:

Why does everyone else have the things I want? (and if I want to really pile on) *I'll never have what they have or have achieved. So I'll just sit here and stew in my jealousy.*

CHAPTER 8

Why Is Life So Easy for Them and Not Me?

For a long time, jealousy was a problem for me. Anger and frustration would literally consume me. I remember this time when a friend of ours bought a beautiful house and threw a big party to celebrate. Walking in that door, into a home that was five times the size of ours, at a time when we had little kids and could barely pay our mortgage, I thought I was going to self-combust. I was so jealous that I could barely contain it, and I did what too many of us do: I aimed it right at my husband. On the ride home, we got into a big fight because I started crying over the fact that "We'd never have a home that nice."

I had this toxic belief that if someone else has what I want, it means I will never have it. I didn't understand jealousy or how to use it to my advantage, so it just triggered all my insecurities. If you live your life in constant, unrelenting, grinding comparison to others, always finding yourself wanting, you will never be able to see yourself as capable of making it happen too. Other people will be the heroes while you sit on the sidelines, watching what they do. This is one reason jealousy can be so depressing if you allow yourself to wallow in it. I want you to know how extremely useful and important it can be too.

Here are some things I hear people say when they feel jealous:

Everyone is winning at the game of life, and I'm always left holding the crappiest hand. It's not fair . . . I'm so sick of hearing about everybody else's fast metabolism, relaxing vacations, fancy home renovations, and amazing dogs who don't chew the couch . . . I wanted ALL that.

Oh! Here she is again with her "I've lost the weight and I've got it all" posts . . . If I had a trainer, I'd look like that too . . . If he says "It's so easy for me" one more time . . . I had the idea to start Uber 10 YEARS ago. I was getting around to it . . . It's so much easier when you don't have kids . . . If only my husband understood me . . . I've had a much harder life, and I don't go flaunting it . . . Anyone can use a social media filter, try showing up IRL looking that good . . . Everyone is outdoing me and there's no room for me to shine.

It's all over for me. I realize, now, that I wanted their success to be MY success. But they've grabbed all the success and it's too late for me to win. I'll just sit here and stew in my inferiority.

The truth is, at one point or another, everyone has felt like the dream version of their life was stolen from them (and for good reason, which you'll find out at the end of this story).

With this kind of self-talk, we mentally shut the doors to what we want because someone else already did it. We give up on ourselves. Jealousy takes over and instead of cheering for the life you want, you start the death spiral of horrible thoughts and feelings about yourself.

I want you to understand that jealousy is an indicator that you can and *should* have that thing you are craving. I'm going to give you some tools to switch your mindset so you can become more excited about your future and have the strength to build the life you want.

But first, I want you to take a good look at how you perceive success. Do you believe success, happiness, and love are in limited supply? I believed that for a long time, and it kept me stuck. I thought that if there's only so much success and happiness to go around, there isn't enough for me.

Once I understood that happiness and success are limitless and they are for everyone (*everyone!*), I began to build the courage and conviction that I was going to get my version of it. That thought alone loosened the reins for me to stop stewing in my jealousy and start doing the work to get what I want.

All our lives we're told, "Don't be jealous" like it's something to be ashamed of—as if it's unseemly, petty, and wrong. But jealousy is simply blocked desire. If you could flip that jealousy into inspiration, the block would disappear. If you could celebrate jealousy as a sign of your next big step in life, it immediately lifts the burden of frustration and insecurity you feel, and gets you moving forward with a high five attitude again.

To understand how this whole jealousy thing works and how you can turn it into inspiration, it's only appropriate that we start at the murky swamp of jealousy, self-hatred, low self-worth, and overwhelming self-doubt. Social media.

The truth no one tells you about jealousy.

The other day I was watching our daughter scroll through social media and I asked her, "What are you thinking about?"

She said, "When I go on Instagram, I just look at other people's lives, occupations, and experiences and want to do the same with my own life, but then I convince myself that will never happen for me regardless of how much I want it. And it makes me feel bad about myself."

I then asked, "What is one experience you want to have that you think will never happen?"

She said, "The other day on social media, I saw a video of a girl who moved to an island in Mexico, found a job there, and was now having the time of her life living at the beach."

I said, "Well, that sounds cool. Why don't you go do that?"

She said, "Mom, it's easier said than done. Seeing her made me jealous because I would like to be doing that. I have always dreamed of traveling and exploring, but I wouldn't even allow myself to think about doing what she did, because I guess deep down I thought, *Well that's great for her but I could never do something like that.* I feel like I'm running out of time, Mom. I'm already twenty-two."

When she said, "I'm already twenty-two," my first thought was, *You're kidding me, right?* which, thankfully, I didn't say. My second thought was *I cannot believe how much pressure she's putting on herself already. She's at the beginning of her life. She has all the time in the world, and now is the time to do something amazing like that.* I didn't say that either. I just listened:

"All I want to do right now is be able to travel and work. Traveling is a dream of mine. But all I see are the obstacles and the reasons it won't work. I'm not the kind of person who just does something like that, and I can't see it working out anyway. I look at her living her best life in Mexico and it makes me jealous because that's great for her, but it'd never happen for me."

And then I pulled out one of the best things I've ever learned to say as a parent. I said, "Do you want me to just listen or would you like me to give you my thoughts?"

She looked at me and said, "I want to know what you think."

I told her, "The thing that strikes me the most is how your self-doubt prevents you from even exploring or leaning into your deepest dreams and desires. You know exactly what you want. Ever since you went to Cambodia with your grandmother in the eighth grade, your heart has longed to travel and explore this world. All of those worries and doubts that you have are normal. We all have them.

"As long as you think *It'll never be me,* you won't take action on the things you dream about. It's normal to feel jealous when you see other people doing what you're scared to do. But if all you ever do is THINK about what you want, it's not a dream—it's a wish.

A dream requires action. It demands partnership. It only becomes real when you find the courage to step toward it."

If you can relate to this conversation, here's the simple thing you have to realize if you find yourself riddled with self-doubt: the world didn't say, "You can't have this." YOU did.

Flip It.

You need to learn that all those other people haven't beat you to it. They're lighting the path and could be high fiving you along the way! Look at yourself in the mirror and instead of seeing a loser, see it like it really is: see yourself as your ally in making it happen. Accept yourself as your best partner in life and you will be amazed at the other partnerships you form to get the thing you are burning to have. See the potential in life and you change; you become somebody who can high five your way forward instead of stewing in jealousy. You are literally flipping the block into inspiration to take action.

In any area of your life where you feel jealous, you're going to flip it into inspiration:

> **Current Limiting Belief:** *If somebody else has it, I can't.*
>
> **Flip It:** *Their success is just proof that I can have it too.*

Jealousy is telling you something.

Just for a moment, notice who you're jealous of, someone in your life or someone you admire from a distance. Now think of that jealous feeling as a signal trying to get your attention. Don't turn away from the jealousy you feel. Don't try to hide it, and don't let it scare or shame you. Turn toward it because it is the fastest way to figure out what you want.

Jealousy is a navigation tool, just like curiosity or desire. It is telling you the direction to steer your life. Tomorrow, when you stand in front of that mirror, let that high five symbolize your commitment to work for what you want. To deserve it. And to empower yourself to go get it.

For our daughter, seeing the friend who lived and worked all winter in Mexico made her jealous. That's good. She needs to follow the jealousy because it's leading her toward the thing she desires most. And when you see someone else doing something that you desire, you may feel pain. Most of us let that pain keep us stuck. You must use it to your advantage. Flip it to inspire change.

In our daughter's case, she should message the girl and say, "I'd love to talk to you. I'd love to do what you're doing, and I'd like to learn from you." That's all you need to do to lean toward what you want. That one action alone transforms jealousy into inspiration.

Another thing she could do is go through her social media and start following accounts of people who are traveling the world and working along the way. Seeing more evidence of what you want will help your RAS make that fast change—to know that it *could* happen for you too. Take a step toward what you want and the jealousy will disappear, and what's meant for you will be one step closer to finding you.

Here's how YOU can start to do this, particularly if you're not sure what you want:

Look again at the people in your life. Who are you jealous of?

Maybe you're jealous of their energy, enthusiasm, and positive attitude. Maybe you're jealous of their YouTube channel or the business they've built. Maybe it's their tight group of friends or the nonprofit they started. Maybe it's how they take care of their health, their lifestyle, their authenticity, where they live, or the fact that they are constantly trying new things and putting themselves out there.

Now go deep: surrender to the pull of your desire.

Don't sit and drown in your jealousy. Unpack it. What is it specifically about this person's life or career that makes you jealous?

Normally we allow our jealousy to make us feel insecure. We invalidate ourselves because we see what other people are doing, or what they have, and we make ourselves wrong for wanting it. That's because you don't believe you're capable of making it happen for yourself.

Your friend's kitchen renovation makes you feel bad about your dumpy kitchen, and then that makes you mad at your partner because the two of you haven't prioritized saving money so you can update your house. As I already confessed, this happened to me a lot when Chris and I were struggling financially. Any friend who was buying new furniture, putting on an addition, or taking an awesome vacation made me insanely jealous because I doubted my ability to create those things for myself.

I was so sad as I told myself, "We'll never have a life like that."

Looking back, I can tell you exactly what was going on: It had nothing to do with the house and nothing to do with Chris. It had to do with my desire to be successful enough to afford something that nice, and *my* ambition. And at the time I was not embracing my ambition. I was pressuring Chris to advance his career, make more money, and give me what I wanted. But your desires are your responsibility, not someone else's. If you want financial abundance, being horrible to your spouse isn't going to create it. Looking at yourself in the mirror and being honest about what you want—that's how you get it.

Or maybe your friend's kitchen doesn't trigger you. Maybe it's your brother's health transformation that sends you into a tizzy. He's been documenting it on Facebook, which makes you wish you had started exercising a year ago. At first his posts inspired you, but now you're getting annoyed as you see the weight shedding. You even find yourself starting to roll your eyes at how happy and enthusiastic he seems online.

If you're feeling jealousy and cattiness when you see your brother's posts, it means you want that. You're just blocked by self-doubt. Once you start to see this push-pull of your desires— meaning your desires are pulling you toward it but your doubt or fear keeps pushing it away—you'll start to see it everywhere. You want what's meant for you so badly that it hurts when you're reminded that you don't have it . . . *yet*.

It happens in your career and in business too. For example, you thought your neighbor's new skin care business wouldn't last. She's asked you to try the products so many times that her passion for this is both off-putting and really impressive. If you're being honest with yourself, she looks like she's having a tremendous amount of fun and making a lot of money, and all the new friends she has through this company make you jealous.

Instead of pushing her away, I want you to surrender to the pull of what you desire. There is something about what she's doing that is meant for you. How can you tell? You're jealous. And you're lucky: you've got someone you could pick up the phone and talk to who is on a path that is calling to you. It doesn't mean you have to sell skin care. Maybe if you reach out and call her, and ask her about her journey, you'll learn something in that conversation that gives you a clue about what's missing for you. Just making that phone call wipes away that doubt and flips your jealousy into inspired action.

Or perhaps your last child has left for college and you're now an empty nester. You cherish those years when you were able to stay home with your kids. But now, all of your girlfriends who worked while raising kids make you feel extremely insecure and jealous. Your résumé has a 20-year hole in it, and you have no idea where to begin. Not knowing what to do is not an excuse to not do something. The first thing you need to do is follow that pull and reach out and start talking to those friends, and other people in your life, about this next chapter that you clearly desire to create for yourself.

It's easier to be envious of other people, or judgy of them, than to admit to yourself that there is something missing from your life. If you don't take action, your self-doubt and jealousy will only continue to build. You're meant to do something incredible with this next chapter of your life. That's what is meant for you. Don't allow jealousy to block you. Just flip it into inspiration and go looking for that something.

I'm not giving this advice only to you— I'm giving it to myself.

I used to let self-doubt and jealousy eat me up inside. But now that I know that jealousy is just blocked desire, I understand how to use it to get what I want. It's a normal emotion and there's not a day that goes by when I don't feel a pang of jealousy. It happens almost every time I scroll through social media. Instead of allowing it to fester, I let it pull me toward what's meant for me. In my mind, I say, *Oh, interesting—I'm jealous.* I explore the feeling and turn it into a signal that inspires action.

Right now in my career, when I look ahead of me, the people I'm most jealous of are the ones who have already started and launched podcasts. For example, my friend Lewis Howes, has been hosting *The School of Greatness* podcast for seven years—I am extremely jealous of Lewis. In fact, I have a bunch of friends who have hit podcasts and I'm jealous of all of them. Honestly, too many to list! I never really thought about it before, but I'm surrounded by friends who are podcast hosts.

I'm jealous and then (*tell me if you do this too*), I beat myself up for not having done it . . . yet. My gift is my voice. I am at my best when I am face-to-face with someone, talking about life. That's what I do on stages, that's what I do when I'm coaching you, that's what I do with my audiobooks, and that's what I did as a daytime talk show host. Because of dyslexia and ADHD, writing is the most difficult way for me to create content, but speaking into a microphone is a breeze.

Creating a podcast would be as natural and fluid as drinking a glass of water. I think I would absolutely love it. So why haven't I launched a podcast? It's the same reason my daughter hasn't started planning a trip around the world. The same reason you haven't pursued that dream that's been whispering to you all these years. You want it so badly, but doubt has convinced you *it will never be you. I'm too late. Someone else already took it. I'll be a copycat.*

The truth is, when I write this out, it doesn't make any sense. There is nothing stopping me from pulling out a microphone from my talk radio days, plugging it into my recording system, and recording a podcast. Or just hitting the Voice Memo button on my iPhone and pressing Record. There is nothing stopping me, but me.

I've told myself, *It's too late. I've missed the window. Everybody and their mother has a podcast—there's no way mine will be successful now. With so many people ahead of me on this podcast journey, how do I do something that's different?* I've trained my RAS to show me the reasons NOT to start. Oops. After confessing all this to you, I was curious. How many podcasts are there? I thought, maybe 100,000. I Googled it. Brace yourself.

There are nearly 2 million shows and 43 million individual podcast episodes out there. Two million shows?! You know how I say you can't do a load of laundry without creating lint? You also can't go through your day without having a negative thought. I felt my heart sink when I saw "2 million shows." *Ugh.* When that happens to you, you must imagine yourself wiping your filter so your mind remains open to what's meant for you. Mentally imagine swatting away that *Ugh* and flip it into, "I'm doing it anyway."

Start paying attention to your jealousy and figure out what it's trying to teach you about where your soul is meant to go. If you don't, the jealousy will get stronger, and louder. It's going to eat your spirit alive. Instead of looking ahead at the destination that represents your destiny, you will start looking around at everyone who beat you to it.

Let's make sure that doesn't happen.

Here are a few questions that can help you flip your jealousy into inspired action—because you need that high five:

- *Who are you jealous of?*

- *What is it about these people and what they are doing, or what they have, that calls to you?*

- *Which parts are you inspired by?*

- *Which parts do you not like?*

- *How would you tweak it to make it your own?*

- *What is the negative thought (or thoughts) that have kept you from allowing yourself to pursue it?*

When I ask myself these questions, it's very clear what my soul is trying to tell me. I need to make launching a podcast my #1 objective in the next chapter of my career. The one thing I could do to get started, as soon as this manuscript is finished, is create a launch plan. Then I could reach out to all my friends and ask them for advice. I could take an online course about it. I could register for a podcast industry event.

The second I start taking action, that jealousy will disappear, and it will for you too.

The same thing happened with our daughter. A few days after our conversation, she reached out to her friend in Mexico and started working on a plan. She worked on the itinerary and changed up who she follows on social media so she sees more inspiration. She asked her boss if she could start her job post-college a few months later than originally planned. It was like she drank an elixir: she was suddenly so full of energy and vitality. She used her jealousy as inspiration and started taking real action toward what she wants. And nothing is more energizing than that.

And here's the other cool thing—if you are not willing to do the work to change or make it happen, then you have no right to be jealous. This shows that you have a habit of focusing on what you lack but truly don't want.

What I love about this habit of flipping jealousy into inspiration is that it is simple, but it's also very beautiful. It affirms what I believe is our essential human nature—which is that we are all co-creators in this glorious life. We are all deeply and energetically connected to one another. One person's success can be success shared by all. We are lifted up by each other's achievements and inspired by their example. So instead of being in competition with all those people on the road ahead, you see allies who can help you get what you want. And don't ever forget that as you find the confidence to move forward in your life, YOU become a light on the path for someone behind you who's still blocked.

CHAPTER 9

Isn't It Easier If I Say Nothing?

Guilt is one of the most powerful emotions in the world. If you are susceptible to feeling it, you need to know how to break free. Feelings of guilt are like reins on a horse. Picture your spirit as a beautiful stallion who wants nothing more than to feel its own power and strength and speed. It wants to race across a field with the sun on its back and the wind in its mane. But the reins of guilt are pulling tight, slowing your spirit down, and eventually stopping it where it stands: Someone you love is going to be hurt or disappointed if you want to race in the direction of your dreams. All it can do is obey.

If you train for a marathon, your spouse will resent you.

If you start selling real estate on the weekends, your boss will find out and be angry.

If you move out of the neighborhood, your old friends make you feel like you think you're better than them.

If you take that job in London, your kids will be ripped out of middle school and never forgive you.

It can also sound more subtle, like:

But . . . I'm trying to cut out gluten. All right, all right, I'll eat a slice of lasagna, Grandma . . . Sure, I can take on that extra assignment for you, even though I'm already buried alive with work . . . Am I a bad mother for wanting our adult kids to move out of the house? . . . You want to borrow my pickup truck? Well, um, I guess . . . Am I a monster for not wanting to go to my sister-in-law's for Christmas Eve (again) this year? . . . My kids will wander the streets if I train for a marathon. It's just easier . . . if I say nothing.

Guilt is a killer.

What I find most interesting about guilt is how misunderstood it is. You probably think other people "make" you feel guilty. Not true. The fact is feelings of guilt are SELF-inflicted. Guilt is tied to YOUR values and your emotional triggers. When you "feel guilty" about something, it's because you believe doing or saying what you want is going to hurt someone else or make them upset with you.

The idea that someone else would be mad, disappointed, upset, or annoyed with you—that's what fuels your "guilt." *It's easier not to deal with it* means it's easier not to deal with people getting upset with you. Whether it's feeling guilty for saying "no" to covering someone else's shift at work, or feeling guilty for not including your clingy friend in your cookout, or feeling guilty about wanting to host the holidays this year because your mother-in-law *always hosts Thanksgiving*—you know what YOU want to do. You just don't want to face the emotional fallout that you ANTICIPATE will come with putting yourself and your needs first. Guilt makes you uncomfortable, so you cave.

You want to move to California, but you feel guilty because you know your parents would be sad. You got a promotion, but you feel guilty because Mary didn't get offered one and she deserves it too. You want to go to nursing school, but you feel guilty because there'd be no one who can pick up the slack at home.

I struggle with this too. Learning to let people feel disappointed and still honor yourself is not easy. But you can do it—and it will change your life.

I have a story to tell you about a pool table.

My dad has a hobby of buying and restoring antique pool tables he finds at garage and estate sales. When Chris and I got married, his wedding gift to us was a painstakingly restored Brunswick pool table, built in the 1870s, the same era as an old farmhouse we bought outside of Boston. After we got married, it sat in my parents' basement in Michigan for years because Chris and I had nowhere to put it. As my business was taking off, we were able to put on a new garage with a playroom attached to our house. When I mentioned it to my dad, he was so excited and said, "Great! You'll have a place to put the pool table!" *Wait, pool table??*

Let the people pleasing begin!

Dad paid for pool table experts to come to the house and carefully assemble it; leveling the slate, smoothing out the felt, and attaching the leather braided pockets one by one. The table was gorgeous—and took up half of our new playroom. Apparently, guilt can severely impair your depth perception and ability to measure accurately. The kids played at opposite ends of the room, and the pool table sat in the middle, like the elephant in the room, covered in Legos, because we rarely used it to play pool. As the kids got older and my business started to grow, we no longer needed a playroom—we needed an office. But I couldn't dare to move the pool table.

When your guilt makes you a doormat, everyone looks like a door.

For two more years it sat in the office like a felted aircraft carrier, forcing everyone to walk around it to get from one end of the room to the other. I was running my business out of my home, but there was no room for desks in the "office," so my employees sat at my kitchen island and in the living room.

I wanted the space back, but I (aka: guilt) couldn't move the pool table. Why? Because I love my dad more than just about anyone and I didn't want to disappoint him. I thought of him every time I saw the table. And not living near my folks, I love having things from Michigan in our Massachusetts home.

Living halfway across the country, my parents only visited us a few times a year. I knew he would understand if I moved it, but still, putting it in storage seemed like a slap in the face to my parents who had given it to us with so much love.

Even though I thought about it every day, I refused to pick up the phone and talk to my dad about it. That's because I'm a people pleaser. And the idea of disappointing someone makes me physically ill.

Warning: what I'm about to say will not please you (but you need to hear it).

Pleasing other people is great if that's what you truly want to do and it makes you happy. It becomes a problem when you start betraying your own needs for the fear of other people being upset with you. I'm talking about not disappointing my father right now, but this is so much bigger. As a people pleaser, I will do anything to manipulate your emotional reaction. I use the word *manipulate* on purpose, because I knew it would bother you. People pleasers think they're being "nice."

Nope, we're liars. If you're a people pleaser, you will behave in a way to manipulate what somebody thinks about you. That's why you spend most of your energy curating yourself so that you fit in, or will be liked, or so that no one's mad at you. You are manipulating what people think about you. Instead of just showing up as yourself and making decisions that work for you, you twist yourself (or your renovated playroom, in this case) in knots so that other people won't be upset with you.

Courage and confidence dissolve guilt.

As I used the pool table as a work surface to lay out all the chapters of *The 5 Second Rule* book for editing, it made me realize that if I wanted to teach other people how to find the courage and confidence to take control of their lives, I needed the courage and confidence to talk to my dad.

I was compromising my own needs of having an office, and even my success, because I was too scared to tell my dad how I felt. I needed to call my dad.

Every day I avoided the conversation was another day of feeling conflicted when I walked into my own office. It was eating away at me. This was also not fair to my father. He didn't give me a pool table so that I would feel conflicted. He gave it to me so that I would enjoy it.

Flip It.

So I'm going to repeat something I've already told you: People pleasing isn't about other people. It's about your insecurities. And my deepest insecurity is people being mad at me. A big part of getting to this place was flipping my limiting belief:

> **Current Limiting Belief:** *If someone is disappointed or upset with your decisions, they stop loving you.*
>
> **Flip It:** *People can be disappointed in you, or upset with the decisions that you make, and still love you.*

As a parent with three children of my own, our children do things all the time that piss me off, make me sad, or create a sting of disappointment. It has never once impacted how deeply I love all three of them. Yet, as a daughter, I was still thinking like a child—that my parents only loved me if they approved of everything I was doing.

I wish I could give you something as simple as the 5 Second Rule and tell you that all you need to do is count 5-4-3-2-1 and magically people pleasing will be solved and the sting of disappointment disappears. That's not how life works, because relationships are a give and take. It took me 45 years to have this epiphany that love and disappointment can co-exist, and often do.

A good daughter would never do this.

Difficult conversations happen because you decide it's time to have them. That's exactly what happened for me. One day, I just picked up the phone and called him. I procrastinated with small talk and then told him my truth: "Dad, you know I love the pool table. But my business is growing so much, I need an office in the house."

And he said, "Oh, it'll look great in the office!"

My guilt meter went through the roof. The universe was really turning the screws. I had to go on to explain that I really needed the space for desks. He suggested putting plywood over the pool table to make it a workspace during office hours, and taking it off on the weekends and evenings to play with it. Not a bad idea, but I knew that wouldn't work for the setup I needed.

Now my heart was racing and my palms were sweating. My dad thought I was calling for help with solving my problem, and I was about to admit that I already had a solution that he wasn't going to like.

Hike up your big girl pants. We're goin' in!

I took a deep breath and I told him that I was going to hire professional pool table movers to dismantle his gift with love and care, and put it in a climate-controlled storage unit. And I promised that when I moved the office offsite, or added on to the house or moved into something bigger, the pool table would get its own dedicated room.

There, I said it.

Now, the fallout.

It's okay, I'll walk to my funeral.

Did I disappoint my father at that moment? Yes. Did I feel guilty? Yes. When the pool table movers came to take it to storage, did I feel like the worst daughter in the world? Yes. When my dad came to the house and saw the home office for the first time without the pool table, was he still disappointed? Yes. When I saw the expression on his face, did I feel like crying? Of course. Does he still bring it up? You bet! And in fact, anytime my parents offer to give us anything, my mother chimes in, "Are you sure you're actually going to use it, or are you going to put it in the basement with everything else we've given to you?"

I love you too, Mom. And yes, I deserved that. Even better, I can take it because I know she loves me and she's human, and is entitled to her feelings too. I also know, despite it all, we love one another very much.

Ripping up the good daughter handbook.

The truth is, writing this, I still feel bad for hurting their feelings, because based on the sarcasm, I can tell my mom was hurt too. And even though I've apologized a million times, it stings when you hurt someone you love. I hate disappointing people. So, when I feel these awful feelings, I just let them rise up, I feel my stomach twist, and let it pass. Sort of like a stomach cramp. They call it a "pang" of guilt because it is physically painful. I have, however, learned to stop myself from taking it to the "I'm a bad daughter" or "I'm a selfish piece of sh*t" stage.

One other thing that helped me was reminding myself of my intention. My intention was not to hurt my parents' feelings or be ungrateful. My intention was to build an office and grow my business. Your parents, or anyone who is disappointed in you, are human beings. Let them be human. Give them the space to feel and to say what they need to say. It's okay. This stuff isn't easy.

It's impossible to go through life and not hurt or disappoint people who love you. But consider that when you put everyone else first, it hurts and disappoints YOU. The point of your life is to go through it and feel absolutely everything—the ups, the downs, the gratitude, the guilt, the sadness, and the love. A good life is full of bad days and a loving relationship is full of moments that sting. That's what makes it real, honest, and true.

Just remind yourself that people can be disappointed or even angry with you and still love you. And Mom and Dad, if you're reading this, and I know you are, that new barn/office we're build-ing? It's going to have a fantastic space to showcase and enjoy that beautiful pool table.

I learned a valuable lesson the day I was honest with my dad: as scared as you are to disappoint someone that you love, it's always worth it to be honest about what you need.

This is definitely harder for women than men.

Break free of guilt.

A few years ago, JPMorgan Chase hired me to create a workshop for their business banking unit. The first year, I went to 24 cities and led seminars for small business owners. The second year, we did the same series, but focused on the issues women business owners face. I was in front of almost ten thousand people during the course of those series and had hundreds of one-on-one conversations.

The most surprising thing about these tours was the topic of guilt—how it came up and why. In the events that were more of a mix of male and female business owners, I was never once asked for advice on managing guilt. But at every single one of the women-in-business events, it came up over and over again, especially when discussing dreams and ambitions.

Studies prove this, but it was obvious to me that guilt was 1,000 times worse for women than for men. We throw guilt into our emotional laundry basket like it's an extra pair of socks. We hap-pily take it on. We always have, because it's how we were raised. It never ceases to amaze me how I feel so much guilt when my mom is sad. My brother just shrugs his shoulders.

It doesn't matter what I do for her, it's never enough.

If your mom is a Jedi master at "making you feel" guilty, I guarantee you—she struggles with guilt too. It's a painful emotion because you feel responsible for something bad that happened (*like this morning when I left the house accidentally with the keys to both cars and stranded Chris*).

Mothers and daughters pass guilt like a hot potato. Your mom feels like she's done something wrong and that's why you never call. When you do call, you feel bad that she says "I haven't heard from you in a while" (because she never calls you) but you get frustrated because it doesn't matter what you do. It. Is. Never. Enough. Guess what? She feels the same about you!

We all just want to feel loved and supported. It goes back to our fundamental needs—to be seen, heard, and celebrated. When you don't know how to ask for the emotional support you need, you tend to get it in destructive ways. *Why don't you ever call me? Too busy for your own mother?* She's just seeking reassurance that she still matters to you, because she feels like she doesn't. You are doing the same when you snap back, "The phone works both ways, Mom." And then you wonder why you feel so much guilt for working? It's because YOU are too busy for your kids. Saying you feel guilty triggers your colleagues to reassure you! Hot potato!

Guilt contracts and love expands.

If you think from guilt (*I can't have this, I shouldn't want this, they'll be hurt if I do*), you are damned if you do and damned if you don't. If you think from love, you see the world full of possibilities instead of sacrifices. (*I can take the promotion and still make time for my kid's recital. I can live far away and still love you deeply.*) I can be

Isn't It Easier If I Say Nothing?

an amazing daughter and not call every day. I'm writing about this because it's an issue I struggle with in my own life and work on personally. I don't live close to my folks and miss them every day.

What helps me is staying grounded in what I appreciate and am grateful for, which is how loving and supportive they are, rather than feeling guilt. When my mind goes, *We live a 16-hour drive away*, I talk back: "I'm not thinking about that!" See how fast you can flip it and get your high five attitude back?! Love you, Mom and Dad!

You don't feel guilty?

Time and time again, women ask me, "How do you manage the guilt when you travel so much and have three kids and a husband at home, as you're pursuing your career?"

My answer?

I don't feel guilty. I feel appreciation.

Women always react in one of two ways when I share this flip in my attitude about guilt. They laugh and nod with approval, or they look completely shocked.

And then I add the most powerful piece: I don't feel guilty because I choose not to.

Do I feel sad sometimes when I'm on the road because I miss my kids? Absolutely. I also feel lonely when I'm traveling and I wish Chris were with me. But I appreciate him and how he supports me and our kids by being home while I travel (just like he appreciates me supporting him while he leads his Soul Degree retreats).

It wasn't always this way.

When I first started traveling, I felt guilty all the time. I thought about my career and my ambition in exactly the opposite way from how I do now. I'd wake up in a hotel room alone and feel guilty that I wasn't back in Boston making breakfast. I'd FaceTime my kids as I was racing to catch a flight, and my heart would sink. When they said "I miss you," it was hard to choke back the tears. I felt like I was the world's worst mother because I wasn't there, and I wanted to be, but we had bills and I needed to work.

Keep repeating the story to yourself that you're the world's worst mother (or daughter), and your RAS will start showing you all kinds of reasons why that's true. If I cracked open Facebook, seeing photos posted by all my friends who were staying home or at least working in Boston made me feel like I was a total outsider in my own community.

Guilt can be heavy and difficult but isn't always bad. There are two kinds of guilt: there is productive guilt (who knew?) and destructive guilt. When used productively, guilt gets you to care very deeply about the world around you and your place in it. It builds awareness of how your behavior impacts others. It protects relationships, nudges you toward kindness, and it motivates you to change.

For example, if you keep missing your brother's birthday, feeling guilty is productive if it motivates you to apologize, make plans to celebrate this weekend, and then spend an afternoon putting everyone's birthdays in your calendar so you don't ever miss them again. As Maya Angelou famously said, "Do the best you can until you know better. And when you know better, do better."

But in my case, I wasn't using guilt to inspire me to do better. I was using it like a sledgehammer, battering myself with it. That's destructive guilt, or as psychologists tell you—SHAME.

Instead of saying "My travel schedule is horrible," you say "I. AM. HORRIBLE." My husband, Chris, did this when his restaurant failed. Instead of saying "The business failed," he said, "I. AM. A. FAILURE." There is NOTHING good about it. Shame is like lumpy gravy on that hot potato, and the more your RAS hears you say *I am a bad person*, the more you'll keep seeing evidence that it's true.

If you struggle with guilt, just answer this powerful question: "Is this guilt motivating me to change for the better, or am I just using this guilt to make myself feel bad?"

What do you want your life to look like?

I asked myself this question: What do you want your life to look like? And let me tell you, it's an eye-opener. When you're clear about what you want, you can empower yourself to go get it—and not keep feeling bad about it. And if you don't know what you want, ask this: What do you NOT want your life to look like?

I knew I wanted to follow my dreams and be present for my kids. I wanted to show my daughters what it looks like to have a mom who's out in the world making a big impact, and show our son what it looks like to follow your own dreams while still supporting your partner, like his father does. I also knew I wanted to be traveling less and around more. Guilt was not helping me achieve these goals and dreams.

Life is not an either/or proposition.

You can have a big career AND be a great mother. You can want more AND be grateful for your success. You can be happily married AND want a better sex life. You can be depressed AND run a marathon. You are a layered, complex creature. You are more than one thing. You just need to stop pounding yourself with guilt, identify what you want, and high five yourself every step of the way as you work to go get it.

You don't have to travel 100 days a year. You don't have to work outside the house. You can be physically present and involved in every aspect of your kids' lives, or your aging parents' last years. Wherever guilt is keeping you from pursuing what YOU dream about, stop anticipating the disappointment and hurt, and face it. Feeling bad isn't helping you change. Being honest about what you want and the support you need, will.

I thought about this a lot after meeting with all those female executives who wanted so many things and then held their spirits back when it was time to let them fly. So I came up with a simple habit to teach them to use the pangs of guilt, and I'm going to teach it to you right now. This is the easiest and best way to start chipping away at that destructive guilt that's blocking you from changing your life and give yourself permission to do what makes you happy.

Stop apologizing.

When you feel destructive guilt, you find yourself saying "I'm sorry" an awful lot. Stop saying you're sorry. Start saying *Thank you* instead. Here's why:

1. *Saying "I'm Sorry" is annoying.*

I bet you've got friends like this. I have a person in my life that I absolutely love. And she struggles with guilt. You can tell because she's always apologizing: "I'm sorry to be asking you for a ride. I'm sorry if I put you out. I'm sorry to ask you to do this. I'm sorry to bother you. I'm sorry that I'm vegan, you didn't have to make something special for me, I could have just eaten my napkin."

It has always bothered me and I finally realized why. When someone is apologizing all the time, they make it all about themselves. They are seeking reassurance. And that's the thing about guilt: it is about YOU! You feel like you are doing something wrong or putting people off so you feel "guilty." When you apologize, you are hoping for an "it's okay."

2. *When you say "Thank you," it showers the people who support you with love and appreciation.*

The fact is, people want to support and help you, and they would love it if you stopped apologizing and putting the focus on yourself, and started saying what we all want to hear: THANK YOU.

So the next time your mom makes a vegan entree or stocks the fridge with oat milk, or buys your favorite roses, or picks you up at the airport or dog sits for you, don't say "I'm sorry I'm so high maintenance." Say, "Thank you for always being so considerate and supportive of me. I APPRECIATE and love you."

3. *Saying "Thank you" is how you take your power back.*

It not only puts your emphasis on the other person, it does something cooler: it gives you your power back. You are acknowledging that you do have needs and you appreciate that people see them and help you fulfill them. Once you start doing this, you'll be surprised how often you need to practice it.

When you apologize, you're communicating that you feel bad about yourself. You're saying that you've done something wrong by needing help or support. Now look: if you have done something wrong, then say so. But doing what's best for you is not wrong. When you say thank you, you are celebrating someone else for showing up and supporting you. You're also accepting that you're worthy of celebration and support.

I stopped telling Chris and my kids that I was sorry I was gone so much and instead started acknowledging them: "Thank you for your love and support—it's the reason I can do what I do. Thank you for helping me pursue my dreams." And then I would tell them

something really cool that happened that day so they felt connected to my work and its impact. Acknowledging and feeling their
love and support expanded me in ways I couldn't have imagined.

4. *"Thank you" is a high five.*

When you say thank you, you share in the celebration of the
people in your life, and yourself!

There's another benefit: you model a high five attitude for your kids.

Guess who showed me what it's like to march toward your
dreams unapologetically? My mom. I love to tell this legendary story
about my mom and how she went after her dreams—on her terms.

It was the summer of 1981, and my mother and her best friend,
Suzi, decided to open up a retail store in downtown Muskegon,
Michigan. They needed capital, so they visited our town's small
local bank, where they were both customers, and they asked for a
retail loan of $10,000. They were excited because they had signed a
lease for the store and had big plans to go to the gift show in Chi-
cago and start buying inventory. When they sat down with the
bank manager, he looked over both of their financial statements
and agreed to approve the loan . . . as long as their husbands would
sign it.

Without skipping a beat, my mother pointed out that she not
only had her own account and was a co-signer on every joint
account, but her name was also on the title of the house that we
lived in, which was going to secure the loan. The bank manager
insisted on the co-signing. My mom didn't feel an ounce of guilt.
She got up, walked over to the teller, and promptly closed every

single account my parents had in the bank. Then she walked out. She got her loan on her own at a new bank. Go Mom!

It reminds you that the first loyalty you have is to yourself. Not a bank, a spouse, a child, or your parents. And the faster you put yourself first, the faster you teach everyone around you how to do it too. My RAS now shows me all kinds of proof for why there is no reason to feel guilty about pursuing my dreams while Chris pursues his. Instead, I feel glad. I no longer see evidence that "I'm a bad mom." I see our kids going after their goals and dreams just like their father and I do.

It's easy to forget that it feels so damn good to help someone else. Thanking the people who are supporting you honors them and makes them feel great. So show a little love to yourself and the people in your life. Live your life. Allow people to feel what they feel and shower them with appreciation. That's how you ditch the guilt in favor of a high five life.

CHAPTER 10

How About I Start . . . Tomorrow?

When you are worried you might fail at something, or are afraid to start, you tell yourself:

I'm not ready yet. It's not the right time. I mean, maybe it could be the right time, but it doesn't feel like the perfect time . . . You know what? I need a full block of time to do this, and I better not start since I don't have two hours . . . Maybe I'll just empty the dishwasher, do a little laundry, rearrange my desk, oh, and push back my cuticles, and take the schmutz out of my belly button before starting. I promise, I'll totally tackle that this afternoon. No, tonight. Tomorrow? Next week . . . next month . . . next year. Maybe another load of laundry first . . . I think my eyebrows need waxing . . .

This is the stuff that goes through my head and maybe yours too.

In this story below you'll meet Eduardo. He's got a big dream, like most of us. He's putting off his big dream because he's not quite ready, like most of us. He's going around and around in circles in his head. If we could get into Eduardo's head (which I did on an Uber ride), it would sound something like this:

My plan to be a famous actor is so inspiring and so amazing . . . but for right now, I need to pay the rent. I mean, I'm making good money at this job, so I can't quit. I gotta be realistic, right? Yeah. I'm going to keep driving this Uber until I feel the moment is right to make my move on the acting scene. And hey, maybe some big producer will come into my car and make all my dreams come true. That's a great idea! Well, it's not actually an idea, it's kind of my plan. It's my only plan. Listen, chasing my dream is not something I can do right now ... I have to pay the bills. But I'm going to achieve my dream. You just wait. One day, I'm going to be absolutely famous. Just not today. Maybe next month ... next year ... It's not that I'm scared or anything. It's just not the right time ... besides, I've got another load of laundry to do.

Procrastination and perfectionism are the two deadliest dream killers. They aren't a high five—energetically, they're a hell no! They slowly choke your ambitions to death until one day you wake up disappointed and resentful when you realize, *I never even got started.* First, let's get one thing straight: You're not a procrastinator or a perfectionist or an overthinker.

You're just scared.

When you catch yourself procrastinating or focusing on being perfect, you've got to flip your mental paralysis into making physical progress, or you're going to be thinking in circles, or in the case of my next story, driving in circles, for years.

"I'm fighting harder for his dreams than he is."

Let me introduce you to a guy named Eduardo. Two years ago I landed at the Dallas airport and got into an Uber. I barely had a moment to say hello to the driver before my cell phone rang. It was one of the executives from Sony Pictures Television calling about the launch of my talk show.

When I hung up the phone, Eduardo introduced himself and said, "I cannot believe you are in my car. I've got to talk to you."

I said, "Oh yeah? What do you want to talk about?"

He said, "You seem like a really cool lady. And I think you can help me."

"That's an awfully nice thing to say. I am a cool lady. If I can help you, I will," I said. "What can I help you with?"

"I want to know how to become an Oscar-winning actor who will create opportunities for Black and Latino men in the inner city who want to be actors."

"Oh, I love that," I said, and then immediately asked him the most obvious thing that was on my mind: "So why are you in Dallas? If acting is the game you wanna be in, you've *got* to be in New York or LA."

He paused. "Right . . ."

"How old are you?"

"Twenty-five."

"Cool. You have two choices," I said. "You either stay in Dallas or you move to where the action is. And if you're 25 years old, I'm going to assume that like the 25-year-old me, you don't have a house and you don't have a spouse and you don't have all the obligations that the 50-year-old Mel Robbins has, so you've got nothing tying you down. After you drop me off, you should give two weeks' notice on this job and you should move to New York or LA."

"But I've only got seven hundred bucks to my name," he said.

"Seven hundred bucks," I said. "Excellent. That'll get you there. Where are you going to go? LA or New York?"

He paused and then said, "I have one friend in LA. Her husband is a graphic designer on movie sets."

"Well," I said, "there you go. That's your in. If the seven hundred bucks gets you out there, why don't you drive for Lyft or Uber out there? Call your friend and say, 'I need to move to LA. I need to stop stalling on my dream. Can I live with you and your husband and sleep on your couch for a couple of weeks while I figure this out?' Worst-case scenario is you blow through the seven hundred, you can't make it work, and you move back here and now you're even hungrier to create it yourself and find your squad in Dallas. But you've got to at least go for it because there's nothing worse than regret. And not moving to California will be something you regret for the rest of your life."

"Got it. I received your advice."

"I hope you do more than receive it. I hope you take that ball I just tossed to you and you run." He laughed. This is the part of our conversation where I started to think, *Why is he laughing? This isn't funny. This is sad. I'm fighting harder for his dreams than he is.*

Your inaction is torturing you.

I've been coaching people for a decade, and I'm telling you, there are two kinds of people: People who see obstacles and people who see opportunity.

A high five attitude is action oriented and sees opportunity. Better, it *creates* opportunity. I'll also tell you that in some situations, like this one, it's easier for someone like me to sit in the back seat and spot opportunities for someone like Eduardo, and be annoyingly positive while he sees nothing but the very real circumstances that are in his way. The magic of the RAS is that we both see the same thing: $700 and a dream. To me this means "LET'S GO." To him this means, "I'm stuck."

That's why you can tell within a few minutes whether someone is all talk or they'll take action. It has nothing to do with a person's conviction and everything to do with their RAS. They're either talking about the obstacles, like only having $700 in the bank, or they're teeing up opportunities, like having a friend who lives in LA they can stay with.

In this conversation with Eduardo, *I'm* the one who has a high five attitude, and all this guy can talk about is what's stopping him from pursuing his dream. That's because my RAS isn't blocked. When Eduardo tells me his dream, my attitude is a total high five. Eduardo, on the other hand, has all kinds of crap built up from his past. He's been telling himself for so long that he'll never make it as an actor that his brain is now programmed to spot reasons why he can't take action and work for it. This dream is barely on life support because of his mindset. The man needs the High 5 Habit.

This isn't just about a 25-year-old Uber driver scared of moving to California. I've coached thousands of people one-on-one, I've talked to hundreds of guests on my TV show, and I've read letters from the millions of people in my online community every day. If you're asking yourself why Eduardo is so blocked, here's the answer: for the same reasons YOU are blocked.

Deeply wanting something in your life can be terrifying.

That's why you think about it all day long but from a safe distance. You stare at it, longingly, but you don't dare move toward it. It's all so painful. I know. Because this used to be me. I can sell anyone anything because I can talk about a big game. But there were many years in my life when that was all I could do because I hadn't yet figured out how to take action when I was scared. I have felt the pain of knowing what my goals are and doing nothing about them because I was frozen with fear, just like Eduardo. You think you're protecting yourself with all this overthinking and procrastination, but the truth is, your inaction is torturing you.

I know you have it within you to take the chance to change your life. The thing you're afraid of might not be as scary as moving to California. It might be sitting down and putting together a résumé and cover letter after spending five years out of the workforce because you were caring for your kids and aging parents. Your mind sees all change as a threat. That's why you're scared of taking a chance.

I'm going to keep hammering the details on this story because catching yourself in the trap of overthinking is very difficult to do. It feels so safe to stay where you are. As you read this story about Eduardo, I guarantee you, you can see how Eduardo is stopping himself. It's easy to see when someone else is doing it. Just like it's easy to see when someone you love has self-esteem and self-worth issues. The real trick is catching yourself.

You and Eduardo need to Flip It.

Let me prove it to you: stop reading for a second and think about something you want to change, try, or do in your life.

Say it out loud.

Maybe it's something you've given up on a long time ago but it's still there in the back of your mind, like my dad's desire to hike the Appalachian Trail, which has been his dream since he was an 18-year-old Eagle Scout. Maybe it's something you're just curious about or you feel drawn to but you don't know why. You haven't given yourself permission to want it. And you haven't trained your RAS to spot opportunities—heck, you might not have even tried to find a heart rock yet (busted!). These tools only work when you use them.

You have been in the habit of denying your dreams. Get out of that habit by realizing your dream is closer than you think. You can use my cheat sheet:

Current Limiting Belief: *It's not the right time for my dreams to come true.*

Flip It: *If I put in the work, I can make this happen.*

Now, as you continue to read Eduardo's story, I want you to have that dream of yours front and center in your mind. Because it's great if this book entertains you, but I want to do something deeper and more lasting. I want it to inspire you to take action. So pay close attention because I decided to give Eduardo some of my high five belief, using one of the simplest mind tricks there is:

Give yourself a deadline.

A deadline means you're serious. One of the coolest things about the High 5 Habit is, it says "Let's go." As in, right now! It sends you back into the court or field. When you look YOURSELF in the mirror and commit to a deadline, the game begins. When you set a date, you yank the goal out of your mind and plant it in the physical world. Your dream and the change you are making becomes true.

"So when are you moving?" I asked.

"I'm giving it a year or two," he replied.

"What? *You're giving it a year?*" I practically yelled it out.

"Yeah . . ." he said.

"I thought you said you received my advice and you were going to move. A year? What? What kind of craziness is that?" I replied.

"Is that crazy?" he said.

"Yes, that's nuts. You're twenty-five years old. What are you waiting for? Get out of Dallas."

"I guess my thing is, I was hung up on money. 'Cause I know that California is expensive."

"How do you know? You don't live there. Call your friend. And investigate whether or not it's actually an issue. It's a simple conversation. 'Can I stay at your place for a couple of weeks? I'm pursuing my dream of being an actor. I only got seven hundred bucks. I can't pay rent. Could I possibly do that? Can I sleep on your couch?' And once you have that conversation, you'll have your answer. And then get your butt out there and find a job, and make your way. That's how you get in the game."

"All right."

"When are you moving?"

"As soon as possible."

"'As soon as possible.' Give me a real deadline."

He said, "What should I say?"

"You need a specific date so you can stop thinking about what you're going to do and start taking steps to make it happen. Give yourself a deadline. This is your dream, not mine, Eduardo!"

I could feel him thinking.

"Eduardo, the clock is ticking. You're only going to get older with each day that goes by. You have so much life to live—I don't understand what you're waiting for. It's mid-September. Make a commitment to yourself, *not to me*, that you're going to move by the first of October. That gives you three weeks to get ready. And so help me God. If I ever get in another Uber in Dallas and you're the one driving it . . . you are in deep sh*t, Eduardo. You may give up on yourself, but I'm not going to. Not when it comes to your dreams. You have until October first, young man."

Now I'm talking to you.

Maybe the problem is you've been forcing yourself to just rip the Band-Aid off. Maybe being tough with yourself is keeping you stuck in place. Try encouraging yourself by giving yourself a little time to get started. To prepare. To take micro actions every day. Think about something you want to change. It could be improving your marriage, or starting a fitness program, or changing your job, or embarking on a project that you've been procrastinating on, or reinventing your life. Now, set a deadline for when that game will start. The deadline creates certainty and gives you something else to focus on: preparing yourself.

One of our daughters used this to manage her fears about going back to school after coming home due to anxiety. She said, "I think that for a long time I wasn't ready to go back. I was trying to force myself to make that change, so instead I just decided to set a deadline in the near future. That gave me a lot of wiggle room to start a routine, have some consistency, get my classes in order so then by that deadline, I've already set in stone all of these healthy habits, instead of jumping the gun and trying to go back before I feel confident in where I'm at. Then once I move back to school, it's just a location switch that's happening instead of a whole mental pattern shift."

By putting a date out in the near future, you take control in a way that helps you feel stronger. And importantly, you give yourself a runway to take off from. You give yourself time and space to gather momentum as you take small daily steps toward that goal. You set yourself up for success. Use that runway, that reasonable time frame, to begin practicing the small changes every day that prepare you for this. High fiving yourself is one of those small changes that supports your choice to make the brave change in your life.

If you've been avoiding a big change because you're scared, let's set a deadline. I suggest three weeks from now. It's enough time to make a mini-plan for what you're going to do between now and then, practicing the small changes every day that prepare you for this so you can take off with the strength and speed of a 747 when the deadline hits.

I asked Eduardo again if he was ready to commit to moving to LA in three weeks on October 1. "Yes," he answered. There was something about the way he said "Yes" that bothered me. His heart wasn't in it. So I said, "You know, it's not my dream. It's yours, so why the hell am I the one fighting for it, Eduardo?"

"Yes. Yeah, that's my dream. I know I can do it."

His voice cracked. Something inside him shifted. He started wiping his face and choking back tears.

"I know you can do it too. You just have to make the decision and DO it. You've got to get out of your head and go for it. Because guess what—this job in Dallas will be here for you if you decide California's not for you. If you hate California, come home. If you don't like it, you can try something different."

Now the tears were flowing.

That's what happens when you stop overthinking. When you clear the block and let inspiration, hope, and dreams flow freely, you'll feel an emotional release. It's cathartic. What happened in Eduardo's mind was that for just a second, all the excuses were cleared away. With a clear and open mind and a high five attitude, Eduardo could see himself in California. He could see himself working hard, sleeping on couches, and auditioning. He could see himself as an actor. He could even see himself winning an Oscar. He could see himself becoming the person he's always wanted to be.

When you allow yourself to just feel how much you want that dream for yourself, it's an overwhelming sensation. You might feel a wave of heat flood your body, you could get all tingly, all the noise around you might quiet, and yes, when you're really in the moment and you realize that your dream is in fact possible and that you're the only one who's holding you back from taking a chance on yourself, you might just cry like Eduardo was crying. Remember that when I asked you to think about a dream of your own, I asked you to say it out loud. Now I want you to take a moment, right here, and allow yourself to FEEL how much you want it. And how much you deserve it.

Ask yourself, "What do you want your life to look like?" and take a moment and just picture it. See yourself doing the work to make it happen. When you allow yourself to feel the change you want, now it's real. When you get upset about something like that, it means you've allowed yourself to believe that it's possible. You felt hope. You realize that you do have a choice!

That's what those tears are about. It's your inner confidence saying, *You are capable. You can do this!* And you probably got honest about how often you have given up on yourself. And there's only one thing that's going to change that. It's taking a chance. You must take a risk and bet on yourself and go for it. And if you think about it, that's exactly what a high five says: *take a chance—let's do this.*

I said to him, "Every day that you sit in Dallas, doing nothing but thinking, you feel like a failure. Fear is winning. You weren't put on this planet to drive other people around. You are an actor, and you know it. Driving is a way to make money right now. But that's not your calling. Do both. Drive cars and act. But you're not acting at all, and that's why you feel so lost. You have turned away from the path that's meant for you. You are disconnected from yourself. You're not only ignoring your calling—you're arguing against it in your mind.

"Every day that you tell yourself you need to wait another year, your brain believes it and you'll be less likely to take this chance. You'll see more reasons not to go and then you'll look up and be thirty-one, and then you'll look up and be forty-seven, and you're still going to be here in Dallas. And for that entire time, you will feel like a failure because all you did was think about all the reasons you can't have the thing you want most in life. Imagine what would happen if you learned how to cheer yourself forward to LA instead of holding yourself back here in Dallas.

"So, Eduardo, you must start to train your mind to spot all the opportunities that are right in front of your face, rather than the obstacles. Can you give me one thing that happened today that is evidence that you should move to California?"

"This conversation right now."

The opportunities are right in front of you.

Now, I want YOU to take this story a step deeper for yourself.

Let's train your mind to stop looking for obstacles and start spotting opportunities. It's easy. All you have to do is write down coincidences, signs, and evidence. It's exactly what I'm about to tell Eduardo to do. This exercise builds on the "Look for Hearts" game you've been playing. Only now, we're going to let your mind help you get what you want.

Let me explain. Have you ever gone on a road trip? Let's say you're driving to Denver and when you first get on the road, you pass a mile marker that says Denver is 400 miles away, then the next thing you know, you pass one that tells you your destination is 325 miles away. Then you're getting closer, it's 215 miles, and then you're so close, only 75 miles. Those mile markers are guide-posts telling you that you're on the right path and helping you clock your progress. You can find mile markers all day long in your own life: they're everywhere around you, helping you count down the distance between you and your goals.

Right now, your RAS is blocking all the evidence that's right before your eyes. Keeping a notebook and jotting down "the signs" pointing toward your dreams changes your RAS and helps you build self-confidence faster.

Here's what I told Eduardo to do:

"I want you to get a notebook, a pad of paper, a journal. Carry it with you. Every time you see a piece of evidence, a sign, a coincidence, or some positive spin on why you should move to California, I want you to write it down in your notebook. I want you to start playing a game where you are pretending that the universe is leaving you clues everywhere to encourage you to go to California."

By writing it down, you are training your mind that this goal is IMPORTANT.

You're activating something called the Zeigarnik effect by writing it down, in which you literally create a mental checklist that the bouncer in your mind holds on to. So every time you write down something that you see as a sign or evidence of something that encourages you toward your goal, you are training and reshaping your RAS in real time.

As I mentioned, this training builds on the habit of looking for heart-shaped, naturally occurring objects. When you tell your mind to look for heart shapes in the world around you, you're creating mental flexibility. It's such a cool way to experiment with your mind. When you get a notebook or a journal and commit to writing down any and all "signs" that you see related to your dream, you're taking this mental flexibility and the training of your mind to the next level.

I continued on with Eduardo: "So tell me, when are you moving?"

"October 1," he said.

"Excellent. Now that sounds like a man who's on a mission. Get your plan in place and move October 1. Okay?"

"Yes . . ." he said.

Now I want to pause with this story for a second. Reading our conversation, it's probably clear to you what Eduardo should do. In fact, you may be screaming at him like I was: "Move to California! What's wrong with you?!" But here's the thing: what's obvious to other people is often the hardest thing to see in your own life. Remember the story about my daughter who thought she was the ugliest one in the bar? Easy for you and me to see that she's just blocked by a limiting belief. Hard to see your blocks on your own.

Your turn.

So, I want you to start playing around with your RAS. At the moment, your RAS is focused on obstacles that are in your way (*no time, no money, not sure where to start, I feel guilty, I'm worried, I feel like a fraud because I've never done this before*).

Let's wipe it away. First, commit to high fiving yourself in the mirror for five days in a row with me at High5Challenge.com. Even if you've already done it, how about we do it together again, this time with me cheering you on with this goal in mind?

Next, set a deadline. Three weeks from now, you get started. Join the gym. Start therapy. Quit the job. End the relationship. Call a Realtor to find a new apartment. Start writing that novel. Start a new healthy habit. During the next three weeks, build a runway and start preparing. Every day, high five yourself forward and just take one step at a time getting yourself ready.

Who could you call? What emails could you send? What risks could you take that you've been avoiding? Who could you ask for help or advice? If you don't know how to do something, is there a book, blog, or YouTube video that could help you?

And finally: get a notebook. Each day, start training your RAS to look for evidence, signs, and synergies that tell you working on this project is the right thing to be doing. Make it a game and write down all the evidence that your dreams are alive and sending you signals.

It's a sign.

So getting back to Eduardo. He knew our conversation was a sign, and here's what I told him:

"Exactly, Eduardo. When it comes to your future, I'm the closest thing to that agent you've been dreaming about. I work in Hollywood, Eduardo. I have a daytime talk show. I'm going to tell you the truth. Nobody is going to find you. I am willing to bet that you have a fantasy in your mind that one of these days you're going to pull up to DFW Airport and the person who gets in the car is an agent in Hollywood who magically gives you a big break. It's not happening. The universe put me here instead. That's why you are getting a kick in the ass and the brutal truth.

"As long as you're sitting here behind the steering wheel, you think you're not going to get hurt. That's where you're wrong, because every day you wake up here in Dallas and you climb into this car and you drive other people around and you think about your dream, you're slowly dying inside. Your spirit is suffocating. All this thinking, and all this waiting, and all this critiquing— they're killing you.

"It doesn't matter how good an actor you are if you never get your butt out of Dallas, take a risk, and get to California. It doesn't matter how funny you are or how talented you are if you refuse to step into the game. The game is not acting. The game is showing up. The game is hearing no. The game is showing up again, and again, and again. That is the REAL work of being an actor. It's now or never. Make your move. Do you want to play that game?"

Eduardo said, "I want to play that game."

"Awesome."

"I want to play that game," he said again, animated. "I'm giving notice and moving to LA."

"You better thank me when you win that Oscar, ten years from now."

"I will," he said. "That's the crazy part. The crazy part is I'm the type of person who will remember this conversation."

"Well, you'd better thank me, 'cause I'll remember it too."

A few minutes later, we pulled up at the hotel. I gave him a hug and waved goodbye as I walked into the lobby, shaking my head. The only thing that was stopping him from pursuing his dreams was himself, and you are doing the same thing.

Now, this amazing conversation happened two years ago. And you may be wondering: Did he move? I don't know. He probably didn't, or maybe he did, but it's beside the point. I tell this story to illustrate that every day you have a choice. You can turn toward the pull of your dreams or argue against it. Fighting that desire inside you and telling yourself, *It will never happen for me* create so much tension in your life.

The point of the story is that there is something meant for you that you will only find when you allow that dream to pull you through your fears. In every dream worth pursuing, the odds are against you. And it doesn't matter one bit that they are, because I know that you would regret for the rest of your life if you play it safe and don't go for it, whatever "it" is. What I've learned the hard way is that having the courage to pursue your dreams is way more important than actually achieving them. That's because it's the act of trying that honors what's truly inside you.

It's why it doesn't matter what happens to Eduardo once he's in LA. What matters is that he believes in himself and moves there. What matters is that he trusts in his ability to figure it out. He forges the resilience that can only come from stretching himself and taking a risk.

What matters right now is what YOU do with Eduardo's story. You've got your own version of "Move to California." Here's mine: it's called "Launch a Podcast," and that's why I can feel Eduardo's pain. And once I launch a podcast, there will be a new thing that I'll start overthinking and be scared to take on. People I'm jealous of. It's all just fear and blocked inspiration—like a bird trapped in a cage. Only action can set that bird free. This is the game of life, so you might as well jump in and play.

Failure is what happens when you give up.

I think the reason this conversation happened was not so Eduardo would move to California but so I would have an example I could share with YOU that is so crystal clear, visceral, and relatable that you would feel sad and infuriated thinking about him not moving. Maybe his stubbornness and fear are the gift you need to wake you up to yours.

When you sit there like I did and you get mad and frustrated with Eduardo, I hope it makes you think about the ways you're holding yourself back because you're scared. Doing nothing is a decision. Waiting is a decision. You think chasing your dream is the risk. You're wrong. The greatest risk is always doing nothing. Because if you fail, you can always go back to what you're doing right now. And based on research, if you fail you are twice as likely to be successful the next time you try. (I guess that explains my success!)

You are Eduardo. You have a dream that you think about all the time, while you're driving a car, or standing in the shower, or sitting at your desk, or reading this book, or washing the dishes, or walking the dog. Just like Eduardo you're thinking and waiting—for the perfect time, or for someone to discover you or give you permission. You're waiting until all the things line up. Waiting to be ready. All that waiting is killing your dreams.

What deadline do you need to give yourself?

Can you commit to a date right now? In the next three weeks, turn yourself toward what you want. Can you take out a notebook and start writing down the evidence that it is meant to be? Can you visualize the steps that lead you there?

Eduardo felt it was a sign that I stepped into his car, so let's call the fact that you're holding this book in your hands a sign that it's time for you to wake up and start changing your life. That happens the minute you choose to do it. Every day you can wake up, look yourself in the mirror, and high five yourself forward. Or you can say "Ugh," and keep driving in circles. I hope you take the wheel in your life, turn it in the direction of your dreams, and cheer yourself forward.

I believe in you. I think you're capable of making it happen. But it's going to be up to you. You will always have a million excuses not to do it. Not to feel like it. Not to believe in yourself.

The only thing that matters in your life is the actions you're taking. The more consistently you take action, the faster you will start to believe in yourself because you will see proof that you are not the kind of person who sits around and feels unworthy. There is no perfect time, perfect plan, or perfect moment. There is only right now, and you're right on time. But time is ticking. As you drive around and think about the life you want, that dream gets shoved further and further into the back of your mind. It's not leaving you, but it is starting to haunt you.

Your dreams are your responsibility. No one is coming.

If you are sitting in Dallas, dreaming of being an actor and waiting for an agent from California to find you, no one is coming.

If you are lying on your couch in London, waiting for someone to set you up on a date, no one is doing it.

If you think about growing your business in Sydney, and you're waiting for your first client to magically appear and buy skin care from you, it's not happening.

If you want a new future, act like it. No matter how scared you are, just start. Wake up every day and high five the person you see in the mirror. Then, set a deadline and get started.

CHAPTER 11

But Do You Like Me?

Fitting in will make you miserable. And you've been trying to do it since middle school. Me too. How about we make each other a deal? Let's both stop caring about being "one of them" and just be *ourselves* and stop giving air time to this nagging question: If I do this, wear this, say this . . . will you still like me? (Or as was the case in my dating life: What do I need to do to GET you to like me?)

When you are an adult, there is only one person's opinion that matters: your own. You've heard that before, and I'm telling you again, because boy, it's hard to get out of the habit of looking around for approval.

Your thoughts, if they are anything like mine, sound like this:

You like monster truck racing? Me too . . . Sure, I'll have another beer if everyone else is . . . I think I better wait a month or two to wear my hair naturally in this corporate setting . . . I don't even like Greek life, why am I rushing again? . . . If I don't own that brand of jeans, sneakers, or handbag, I'll just feel so lame . . . Just another layer of foundation and a bit more bronzer and then I'll look like my friends . . .

Why are we all so insecure?

Blame life. The moment you start school, the driving force of your life becomes fitting in. It's not only social—sometimes it's a matter of survival! We've all had the experience of being that kid in the cafeteria wishing you could sit with a certain group of other kids. If only you could be with that group of girls, if only you were rich enough, or had better clothes, or looked more like everyone around you. If only you had made the soccer team, the musical cast, or the honor roll. If only you were taller, darker, less this, more that. If only you were born smart or athletic or had perfect pitch. Then you'd be okay.

That's how it starts. You start to see the world in groups you belong to and groups you don't. And you start to morph yourself and what you say and how you feel just to fit in.

This is when you stop accepting yourself in the mirror and start rejecting all the things about you: *Teeth are too big. Skin is broken out. Too short. Too big. Too many freckles. Hair is too kinky.* It's when you make the biggest mistake of your life: you decide that you'd rather fit in than be yourself.

We all do it. It's how we survive middle school. There's no escaping it. The problem with this pattern is that you carry it into high school. And college. And work life. And suburbia. In fact, your entire adult life. You tell yourself it's easier to just be like everyone else. Get the job, climb the ladder, settle down, get a dog, buy the house, have some kids, sign up for town soccer. Fitting in as a kid morphs into keeping up with the Joneses as an adult.

And it's not just your habit of looking around and seeing where you fit in. It's that sometimes the experiences of your life make you feel like you don't belong at all. It might have been a death by a thousand cuts. Whether it's a mom who constantly criticized you and micromanaged every aspect of your life. Or a dad who pushed sports or law school down your throat when you wanted to be in the play, the relentless stress of living in poverty, a group of friends who stabbed you in the back, or the constant microaggressions you deal with because you are the only Black person at the office and so you start code-switching to fit into a workplace that makes you feel like you don't deserve to be there.

Whether the message was subtle or clobbered into your head, it was: *It's better if you are liked than being your true beautiful, unique self.* And for you, it might have been safer to fit in, because just being you put you at risk. When you don't feel like you belong, the world feels so big. You start to feel small. And the noise all around you muffles the most important voice in the world—your own.

The connection between fitting in and anxiety.

When you can't be yourself, it creates anxiety because you don't know who you're supposed to be—so you are constantly reading the room and looking outside yourself for cues on how to act and what to say. This puts you in a constant state of being on edge and questioning and rehashing your every move. *Was that sentence written right? Should I have sent that text?*

Women, in particular, struggle with this kind of anxiety. There is a reason for this: women are trained to play roles. You play the role of the good daughter, the little sister, the good student, the team player, the BFF, and the dependable employee. You've always felt consumed by making sure Mom was happy, Dad wasn't mad, your outfit was "right," your answer in class "didn't sound stupid," and when you went to the party "you looked great." As a kid it's normal to worry about whether or not people like you. But the pressure to fit in and fall in line has gotten WAY worse since you and I were kids.

Don't even get me started about prom.

When our two daughters were in high school and old enough to go to the prom, I was shocked and angry to see this tradition where the girls set up a Facebook group and four or five months before the prom, before anybody even has a date, they start claiming which prom dress they are going to buy, even putting dibs on them so no one else can buy something similar. This bizarre ritual reinforces, through an entire school system of girls, the idea that you can't just be yourself. In fact, you can't even buy what dress you want! The message is clear: there's a right way to do something. A right dress to wear or not wear, because heaven forbid you might wear a similar dress to someone else's.

What's worse, if you break this social code, the entire school system will be "mad at you." Nobody stops to think about how absurd it is. My daughters put so much pressure on themselves and me to "get to the mall" because the Facebook group was starting to fill up, that instead of this being a cool memory and rite of passage from high school, it erupted into an anxiety-fueled screaming match inside a dressing room at Nordstrom. We were fighting because my daughter had found the perfect dress, but someone had "already claimed" it (and two other dresses). I objected, "But it's a different color!" She said, "I can't, all the seniors will be mad at me." This, by the way, all happened before she even had a date!

The two hours we spent in Nordstrom will probably result in about three months of therapy where she discusses my anger issues. What I was experiencing firsthand was that my daughter was very clear there was a role she was supposed to play at this moment in her life. She couldn't pick any dress she wanted—it had to be one that fit the criteria someone else had set out. All the anxiety about the dress (and the makeup, the hairstyle, the manicure, the tanning, the limo rental, waxing) is about playing the perfect role.

No wonder none of us know how to be ourselves. We've been indoctrinated into following the social rules forever. And in that gap between "the rules" and who you really are, anxiety seeps in. My daughter and her friends say they're anxious about finding a prom dress, but what they're really anxious about is finding their way in a world with all these rules.

The real question we all need to focus on is not *Will THEY like this prom dress, hair style, career choice, or decision?* It's <u>*DO I LIKE IT?*</u> Imagine the guts it would take to be a junior in high school and to knowingly choose to wear the same dress that someone had "claimed" on some dumb Facebook page. Kids think it would be social suicide.

I think it's the secret to life: doing what works for you and letting people say whatever they want about you.

Because it doesn't matter what other people say. The only thing that really matters is . . . Do YOU like you?

You'll never be able to stop caring about other people's feelings.

If you did, you'd be a narcissistic asshole. You should care about other people's opinions, but it doesn't mean that you have to listen to those opinions. To change your life, you need to learn how to honor your feelings *more* than anyone else's.

You also need to learn how to give people the space to have those feelings and not make it mean anything about you. *(If you have a lot of trouble with this, go back and reread Chapter 9 on guilt.)* This is so important because if you can't value yourself, you will look for validation from other people.

In my life, too many times, I was basically a human chameleon, morphing into whatever kind of person I needed to be in my relationships, especially in my romantic ones. I not only said yes to things I didn't want to do, but I actually pretended I liked stuff that I didn't like, just so I would fit in. (*Hello, Grateful Dead phase.*)

At the very beginning, I said the High 5 Habit is about improving the relationship you have with yourself. This is critical because your relationship with YOU is the foundation for all other relationships. If you feel secure in who you are, you'll be secure in your relationships. You'll be able to draw boundaries, you'll be able to give people space to be themselves, and you'll be able to ask for the love and support you need.

If you feel insecure about yourself, you'll be insecure with others. You'll also insert that insecurity into every interaction you have.

I have a story to tell you.

When I was in my 30s, I dove headfirst into personal development. It was like the time I tried pad thai for the first time. I had no idea what I had been missing out on! Once I had a taste of personal development, Chris and I treated life like a buffet. We signed up for every kind of retreat, training, or life-changing experience we could find and afford.

We learned to meditate and practice yoga, trained to be wilderness EMTs, and took classes on being more productive and communicating better. It was inside these experiences, with a bunch of strangers wearing name tags, that we found our people, and a deeper connection to ourselves, to each other, and to our purpose.

I remember sitting in the audience at Oprah's Live Your Best Life tour nearly two decades ago. The DJ had filled the Boston Convention Center with dance music, and I was up on my feet with thousands of other women, with my name tag on, dancing and high fiving everyone all around me. As we took our seats, the next speaker took the stage. It was Martha Beck, Oprah's life coach. I had no idea who the hell she was. Never heard of her. But as soon as she started talking, everything fell quiet.

I heard myself say, "I want to be doing THAT." I didn't even know what "that" meant, but I can tell you now, "that" was the moment I made the decision to become a life coach. One of the first actions I took was to hire someone to train me, and I found the perfect person in an adjunct professor at MIT's Sloan School of Management who was teaching a course on "life design." I was already volunteering to lead seminars for a life-improvement company on the weekends, but I had no idea how to start my own business doing it.

After about six months of working my day job, getting trained in the business of coaching, and volunteering as a course leader on the weekends, this professor said I was "ready" to start marketing myself to paying clients. I asked her if I could get some kind of certificate, "You know, like a diploma, to show my credentials."

And without skipping a beat, she said the most life coach thing I've ever heard: "You don't need a piece of paper to prove that you're qualified, Mel. You're just scared." I could feel my anxiety rising as she said it.

"Here's your homework," she said. "You've got two weeks to land three paying clients. If one of them tells you they won't work with you unless you can show them your certificate, then I'll go to Staples, get a fancy "certificate" form, and sign it for you. Mel, you've been taking life-improvement seminars for years, you've trained, you've got years of experience coaching, you have a law degree, and you're a trained crisis intervention counselor. You're ready to coach other people. You were ready years ago—you were just afraid. You don't need a certificate. Get out there and go land some clients."

It was just like that amazing pep talk I would give Eduardo 15 years later, and being on the receiving end of it—I hated every minute of it! She was right. I'd been training for years and had worked hard to achieve this dream of mine. The inspiration lasted until I got to a cocktail party that night and someone asked, "What do you do for a living?"

I replied, "I'm a life coach." (*Now, keep in mind this was 2001, when it wasn't really a thing.*)

"A life coach? What the heck is a life coach?"

I froze. This is where that desire to fit in kicks in. (*Please like me!*) I could see the wheels in his head spinning as he thought about the words *life coach*. I remember feeling embarrassed. My neck got hot and my cheeks felt flush. I started to think, *I bet he thinks that life coach sounds like the kind of profession your aunt goes into after she gets sober or what your 23-year-old roommate becomes when she can't get a job right out of college.*

If I'd had a certificate from Staples that said, "Life Coach," I would have pulled it out and handed it to him. But that wouldn't have taken away my fear. The woman who trained me was right. I didn't need a certificate to prove anything. I was already f*cked based on my own insecurities. Whatever YOU are insecure about, and whatever your deepest fear is, you'll project that fear into every single conversation, awkward silence, or text.

You're the one judging you.

Here's the crazy thing about your insecurities and your negative self talk: It's in YOUR head, not theirs. Whatever negative crap you think about yourself, you also think other people think that same thing about you. My biggest fear is that someone is not going to like me or approve of what I'm doing. But here's the most important thing: at this moment, this dude isn't judging me. He's thinking. I'm the one who is judging me.

You do the same thing! You hear YOUR inner critic inside other people's minds. I didn't have a clue what this guy thought about me or the profession of life coaching. I just knew he looked like he was thinking about something, and in moments of uncertainty like this, you automatically project your fears and insecurities onto the other person. If you're afraid of people thinking you're too short, or too loud, or not attractive, or annoying, or weird, or what you do for a living is stupid, then you'll assume that's what that person is thinking too. And one more thing: nobody is staying up at night thinking about you. They're too busy thinking about their own shit. If this guy is as insecure as me, you know what he was thinking? *Am I the only person who doesn't know what a life coach is?*

I can tell you that in that moment of silence, I thought he thought I was a complete idiot and that being a "life coach" was the stupidest thing he had ever heard, and it's what people who can't get real jobs do.

Now, I don't believe that coaching is silly. I think coaching is the coolest thing in the world. That should be good enough for me, right? No, it's not good enough, because what I really want is to be liked. I want to fit into this guy's world. That's why my self-talk started getting judgy: *He thinks it's stupid.*

Guess what? I was so wrong. That's not what he thought at all. After an awkward silence, he asked, "Seriously, I've never heard of a life coach. What do you do?" When I explained that I worked with *successful people who feel stuck*, he replied, "That sounds like me." He ended up being my very first client because his wife was standing next to him and said, "How much do you charge? He needs someone like you."

This story has a positive ending, but there are plenty of times someone has judged or ridiculed me for being a life coach. When I first told a group of girlfriends about my new business, one of them actually turned to me and said, "Life coach? Why would anyone come to you for life coaching?" When she saw my startled expression, she tried to soften the slap in the face she had just given me: "No, seriously, you're not a therapist. How do you even know what to do?"

It's a fair question. And when I removed my own insecurities, I could see why she asked it. I had never talked about my passion project of personal development with my friends because I was afraid of being criticized. She had no idea I had been essentially training to be a life coach for almost five years. We spoke for a little bit longer about my training and my process. A few months later, a friend of hers from college reached out. What I had interpreted as a judgment was merely a question, and it led to a referral.

Flip It.

As you become clearer about what changes you want to make, you'll have moments when you're ready to say, "Screw everybody. I'm going to quit my job, become a life coach, wear the prom dress, live my best life, and do whatever the hell I want." *Double birds to the world!*

This story about networking and my insecurity has a happy ending, but seeking other people's approval goes way beyond wearing the right prom dress or needing a certificate from Staples to validate you. The constant need to be liked and have other people validate your decisions leads you to twist yourself and your life into knots and will keep you in careers, friendships, and marriages that make you miserable.

Current Limiting Belief: *What will everyone think?*

Flip It: *My happiness is more important than what anyone else thinks about it.*

Just ask Katherine. She reached out to me from Ireland, where she was a successful ad executive in an unhappy marriage. She said, "My entire life, I have been doing what I thought I was supposed to do. I went to the best college in Ireland. I got my master's, went to London, got a boyfriend, and got engaged. We were so wrong for each other, but I was ticking off everything you're supposed to do before 30."

Things veered off course quickly in her marriage. Still, she tried everything she could to save it, including going to six marriage therapists. She described their marriage as an "Irish divorce," which she explained, "My husband is in the U.K., while I'm back home in Ireland." She added that none of her friends in Ireland were divorced. She wanted to get a divorce, but the thought of people not liking her decision paralyzed her. When she talked to her mom about the divorce, her mother said, "What about your poor children?" *Thanks, Mom.* Those five words stung so badly, Katherine let another two years pass.

This is why anxiety is intertwined with your insecurity. The anxiety happens for two reasons. First, you never know how to act because your only guide is making sure you aren't upsetting anyone else. And second, it comes from a deep knowing that you are not being true to yourself. Living a lie creates anxiety because you anticipate the massive reckoning that's due when the truth comes out. When you wake up every day and play the role of good daughter, good wife, and hardworking employee, but you hate your life, that's not a high five life. That's its own form of hell.

Everybody had an opinion about who Katherine should be: her mother, her friends, the Catholic Church, and the country of Ireland. They were more comfortable with her being married than being happy. So for six years, she wanted a divorce, but stayed in the miserable marriage. She was living a lie for other people's approval.

A moment of truth.

She said, "It occurred to me one night lying in bed: I'm completely alone with these stabbing pains at night from the stress, and none of these people whose opinions I fear are trying to tuck me in at night. They are not helping me through any of this, so why even care what they think?"

When she went to therapy the next day, the therapist asked Katherine and her husband to imagine their lives two years from now. She separated the two of them, made them stand apart, and said, "This represents your life if you get divorced." Katherine started crying thinking about what her mother and her friends would think.

Then, the therapist asked her to cross the room and stand next to her husband. She then said, "Imagine two years from now, and you're still a married couple." Katherine thought about what she wanted. Would she like to be with him for another two years? She started sobbing hysterically. She asked for a divorce right there and then.

When you like yourself and your life, it might upset your mom, and your kids, and your friends, and your church, and maybe even the country of Ireland. Doing what's right for you will be hard in the beginning. You'll raise eyebrows. You'll be gossiped about. So what. Your life is hard now. People gossip about you now. You are unhappy now. The only thing that you have to lose is the weight of everybody else's opinions and the miserable job or relationship weighing you down. What you gain is freedom, happiness, and most importantly—the rock solid confidence of knowing you put yourself first.

If Katherine's story is making you go, "Uh oh," about some aspect of your life, here's an easy way to know when it's time to put yourself first. When you don't feel like high fiving that partner, friend, lifestyle, job, or situation, that tells you: it's time for a change.

Just ask yourself, at any moment, do you want to high five this? If the answer is no, you have a choice: work hard to change it, or end it to create room for something new.

One change opens up limitless possibilities.

Since her divorce, Katherine has improved just about every area of her life. She not only got out of her marriage, she landed an amazing new career opportunity and bought a house. She told me, "Two years ago, the only thing that got me out of bed was that my kids had to be fed, dressed, and taken to school. Now it's time to look after me so every day I wake up and I get on my treadmill. I'm learning to put myself first and looking back, I wonder, 'Why didn't I do it before?'"

The reason she didn't do it before is because she didn't know how to put herself first. As you learned in the beginning of this chapter, the need to fit in and the desire for approval is so indoctrinated in you, you probably aren't aware of how much it's controlling your day-to-day life.

Change always begins with something tiny, like waking up every day and high fiving yourself in the mirror. When you change how you see yourself and treat yourself, a whole new possibility opens up for your future self. It begins with celebrating YOU and putting your needs first—and that creates a snowball effect in every area of your life. As Katherine put it, "I finally feel that I am the driver of my life."

CHAPTER 12

How Come I Screw Everything Up?

Spoiler Alert: Life is going to test you.

When you're working to change your life, or achieve a goal, or pursue your dreams, you will hit a roadblock. Always. It is unavoidable. You fail the entrance exam. You get fired from the dream job. You get sick. You hear a thousand nos every time you tell someone about your business idea, product line, or book manuscript. You lose the election. Or in the case of this story I'm about to tell you, you make mistake after mistake as you are trying to launch your first book.

When that happens to me, the death spiral of negative thoughts and emotions makes me want to throw my hands up in the air:

Nothing ever goes my way . . . I knew something was going to happen . . . So why should I keep doing this? . . . It looks like I'm failing and it's not working out . . . It's too complicated . . . I did it the wrong way . . . I feel so foolish that I thought it would work . . . I'm always pushing the boulder up the mountain . . . My algebra teacher/kindergarten teacher/ piano teacher/track coach/ex-wife/dad was right—I'll never amount to anything.

That's it. I quit.

How you respond to a moment of failure separates the winners from the losers. Not to be harsh, but it's true. I'll get into that a little later, but for now, I want you to be able to see the sh*t hitting the fan and think, *THIS IS A GOOD SIGN! I must be doing something right.* Trust me. I know a thing or two about messing up. (I literally wrote the chapter on it. See Chapter 14.) And I know how it feels when it seems like nothing works out for you.

When I launched *The 5 Second Rule* in 2017, it was a complete and utter disaster.

It was my first book launch, and I wanted to crush it, so I spent six months studying what best-selling authors do and planning our marketing campaign in agonizing detail. I created presale campaigns, landing pages, and social media marketing funnels. On the day the book came out, I sent my newsletter list links to buy the book online, and to my amazement, thousands of people bought it. Then, within a few hours of sending out the email, I started to get responses:

"Mel, Amazon is showing the book is 'out of stock.'"

For a second I was so excited. I thought we had sold out our entire inventory of books in a matter of minutes. It was beyond my wildest dreams. But as the emails kept coming in complaining my book was "out of stock," I started to realize that I don't have enough people on my email list to sell out, so something must be wrong.

What I now know is that when Amazon gets a surge of orders on an unknown product, they may list it as "out of stock" until they sort out whether the demand is real or a bunch of bots. Sucks for me because it meant my book was unavailable—the entire two weeks of my book launch. You could not buy it if you wanted to.

It has always been my dream to be a best-selling author. On my vision board I cut out images of "#1 *New York Times* Bestseller" and "publishing phenomenon." I imagined being written up in magazines and being called a "disruptor" in the publishing world because I had chosen to self-publish. I was a complete moron. I had no idea that self-publishing means your book is not recognized by most bestseller lists. And it makes the hardcover really hard to find in your local bookstore. The obstacle I was facing was real, but it was my mindset that caused me to crash and burn.

I bombarded myself with negative thoughts: *How stupid could I be? I mess everything up. By the time this gets fixed, no one is going to want to buy this book. Why do I always have to do things the hard way? I should have worked with a publisher. Why do things never work out for me?*

Mentally, I took a nosedive. You've experienced this feeling too. You poured your hopes and dreams into a goal and then you didn't get it. It stings to watch someone else get into your dream school, or land the spot on the starting lineup, or receive the promotion you thought you deserved. It doesn't mean the other person didn't deserve those things, but it's easy to use those moments as a battering ram against yourself. I know I certainly have.

Flip It.

I felt devastated, but I couldn't afford to have a breakdown. I had worked so hard to set up events and podcast interviews that I had to keep going. I had to pick myself up off the ground. So I started telling myself what I needed to hear: *Mel, there is no way you worked this hard and will not be rewarded. You have to trust that there is something amazing happening that you can't see right now.* See how I flipped that?

> **Current Limiting Belief:** *Nothing ever works out for me.*
>
> **Flip It:** *Something amazing is happening that I can't see right now. Keep going.*
>
> **Or:** *When you smell crap, there must be a pony nearby.*

Life sucks at times. When you feel like you just can't catch a break no matter how hard you try, you just have to keep going. This mantra—*"You have to trust that there is something amazing happening that you can't see right now"*—is like your own personal halftime locker-room speech. Have a good cry and then dust yourself off and keep fighting for what you want. If you give up, you give up on you. You must tell yourself that something better is coming and keep going. And in that moment, that's what I did. This is mentally what it looks like to high five yourself forward.

Every day, I assured myself that my hard work would be rewarded, and that something I couldn't see was in store for me, all I needed to do was be patient and persistent and it would be revealed. The more I practiced this high five attitude, the more I believed it.

Tom Bilyeu and my stress diarrhea.

Fast-forward two weeks, and I'm in Los Angeles, about to appear on Tom Bilyeu's YouTube show, *Impact Theory.* I need this interview to go well. By the time this interview gets posted on YouTube for Tom's millions of fans, the book should be available.

I should feel excited. I should be grateful that Tom has asked me to be on his show, but you know how I feel? I feel like I'm going to have stress diarrhea. I feel like something's about to go wrong, because everything else has. And that's why it's critical that you watch your mind like a hawk. Once you allow yourself to worry about one thing, you'll start worrying about other things. Lint is tiny, but it builds.

This interview with Tom is my chance to save three years of work from becoming the biggest professional failure of my life. The stakes feel impossibly high. I excuse myself to use the bathroom. Standing in his bathroom staring in the mirror, I see my armpits are already starting to sweat through my bright red shirt. I'm mortified. My face is so flushed with stress, it's as red as a baboon's ass, and all the foundation at Sephora wouldn't be enough to hide it.

If I knew the high five or some of the other tools you're learning, I would have used them, but four years ago I was still white-knuckling myself through stressful situations. I started imagining myself freezing on camera, forgetting what to say, and making a complete fool of myself. I blot my armpit stains with toilet paper (does not work). I splash cold water on my face to try to bring my fire-engine red cheeks down to a mere flushed look (also does not work). My attempt to make myself presentable is interrupted by a knock on the door: "They're ready for you, Mel." So just as any world-class keynote speaker would do, I look at myself in the mirror, take one more deep breath, and say, "Pull your shit together, Mel." I take one last deep exhale, 5-4-3-2-1, and I open the door.

On the other side of the door, a production intern is holding a clipboard. I follow her through the Bilyeus' beautiful home and make my way to the edge of the talk show set they've built in their living room. Tom and his wife, Lisa, are warm and gracious, and I like them immediately. I desperately want them to like me too. *Deep breaths, Mel. Deep breaths.* As we wait for the show to start, Lisa asks me, "How's the book launch going?" I feel the urge to lie, but I stop myself. I smile and say the truth: "It's been more challenging than I expected, and I really appreciate your support."

Then Tom starts his introduction. He greets his millions of fans who will watch this interview and introduces me using a word that sets my teeth on edge. *Motivation*. As in, "Please welcome Mel Robbins, *the master of motivation*."

He's talking about the motivation that surges when the spin instructor yells at you to pedal faster during the last five minutes of class. Or the motivation you feel when your high school coach gives one of those made-for-the-movies halftime locker-room speeches: *Stop crying! What the hell were you doing out there? Get your asses back out there and win this!* Or the motivation you experience in church when you hear a life-changing sermon that stands the hair up on the back of your neck. Motivation is what bodybuilders eat for breakfast. It's what the Kardashians probably feel when they leap out of bed. Yet motivation is NOT what got me out of that bathroom. I forced myself out.

Of course, when Tom called me "the master of motivation," he meant it as a compliment, and it's not like he's ill-informed or making things up. If you look me up, you'll see that even my Wikipedia page lists me as a motivational speaker, in fact one of the most successful in the world. So there's no way he could have known how much that word—*motivation*—makes me want to vomit.

Here's why: As I said earlier, motivation is never there when you need it. And when you are afraid . . . forget about it. Your body sounds the alarm and goes into fight or flight, sending your mind in the opposite direction of where you need to go.

When I was standing in Tom and Lisa's bathroom looking in the mirror, all I saw was a woman with a failed book launch, pit stains the size of dinner plates, and cheeks as red as a baboon's ass. I wasn't motivated while staring at my pit stains. I wasn't motivated when I tossed cold water on my face. If I had waited to "feel motivated" to save myself, I'd still be in that bathroom worrying that I wasn't capable of acting confident while my book launch was in free fall.

Life is about decisions. When you are faced with scary news, an unexpected bill, the words "I don't love you anymore" or "You're fired," or when your implants have been recalled, or you find a lump on your groin, or you're staring at your reflection in the mirror and you look as worried as you feel—you have a decision to make.

Are you going to stand there and let your worries consume you, or are you going to fight back and take control of your mind? When life knocks you down, you have to find a way to knock back. You always have a choice about what you say to yourself. I could have just as easily looked at my reflection and said, "You're f*cked." I decided to say "Pull your shit together." It wasn't as good as a high five would have been, but it was the slap across the face that I needed.

So despite my armpits and my worries, I gained my composure and walked out onto the set.

As Tom started listing my accomplishments, all I could think about was how bad the book sales had been, and the imposter syndrome I felt at that moment was visceral. I didn't belong there. I wasn't good enough. It felt like being in middle school and being called on when everyone was staring at you. *What's she going to say?*

I thought, *This is preparing me for something amazing. Just be yourself.* I walked out, gave him a hug, and then Tom called me "The Master of Motivation." I laughed at the title and the four words I responded with changed my career:

Motivation. Is. Complete. Garbage.

Tom leaned in. "Why do you say it's garbage?" And then I went off and just said exactly what I believe millions of people struggle with:

"At some point, we all bought into this lie that you've got to feel ready in order to change. You think what's missing is motivation. And that's not true, because of the way that our minds are wired. The fact about human beings is that we are not designed to do things that are uncomfortable or scary or difficult. Our brains are designed to protect us from those things because our brains are trying to keep us alive. And in order to change in any way that really matters—to build a business, to be the best parent, the best spouse, to do all those things that you want to do with your life, with your work, with your dreams—you're going to have to do things that are difficult, uncertain, or scary, which sets up this problem for all of us. You're never going to *feel* like doing it. Motivation is garbage."

Always say what you believe.

Your real opinion is more interesting than what you think people want to hear. Our conversation became one of the most popular episodes of his talk show, gaining more than 10 million views in a matter of months. And then someone turned me into a meme titled *"This Woman Nails Why Motivation Is Garbage,"* and it went crazy viral, to the tune of over 20 million views. And, as far as I know, no one noticed my pit stains.

Because of that viral clip, I went on to do another interview, and another. And then podcast producers started calling. I kept saying YES. Even with all this new publicity, because it was so hard to get the book, sales seemed sluggish. But I watched my mind like a hawk. If I felt myself go low, I just told myself it all must be happening for a reason and kept going.

Thank God I did, because it turned out something incredible WAS happening.

While Amazon was "out of stock," it never occurred to me that people could still buy the audiobook. I had recorded and self-published the audiobook on my own too. We had no idea what we were doing. I recorded it in one sitting and kept in all the mistakes, like shuffling my papers, dropping my pen, and taking a sip of water, because I didn't know any better. My husband uploaded the audio files to Audible, and I took a screenshot of *The 5 Second Rule* book and uploaded it as the cover photo.

Turns out, because it was the only version available, people were buying up the audiobook version of *The 5 Second Rule* faster than toilet paper in a pandemic. I didn't know any of this was happening until about a month later, when I got an email from Audible with the subject line "Your Monthly Report Is Here." When I clicked on the report, I nearly fell out of my car. The sales were through the roof and we already had thousands of five-star reviews on Audible. My first thought: *Maybe we can finally get the liens off our house.* My next thought: *Holy shit, audiobooks?!*

One of the stand-out aspects of that audiobook that readers love is the fact that it sounds like I'm sitting next to you because it's so unedited. I say this to point out to you that every "mistake" I made turned out to be an invaluable lesson AND the secret to my success. For a month, I had been telling myself I was a failure (*which only makes your RAS show you more reasons to think you failed*). That mantra gave me the high five attitude to keep chipping away.

And here's the irony: Had the hardcover been available, I never would have had the landslide of sales on Audible. In fact, *The 5 Second Rule* became the #1 (as in, THE most listened to) audiobook of 2017 on all of Audible. Eventually Amazon got its algorithm sorted out, the hardcover was on sale, and it ended up being the sixth most read book OF THE YEAR on Amazon.

And here's another thing I want you to know:

Despite being a global sensation with millions of copies in print and more than 100,000 five-star reviews (*I'm serious*), *The 5 Second Rule* has never made it to a traditional bestseller list. That proves a point about your goals and dreams that I deeply believe.

The purpose of any dream is to provide the fuel that drives you and the map that shows you the direction to head. It may or may not lead to the destination you think it will—but the finish line is not the point. My dream of making a list is what drove me, but achieving it was not the purpose of that dream.

When you are able to trust that all your hard work is leading you somewhere, you will create miracles in your life. And in some cases (like mine), the miracles you create aren't even the ones that you imagined. I didn't achieve my dream of being a *New York Times* bestseller. Something even better happened. I learned the importance of not giving up. I learned an entirely new and innovative business model as an author. It led to a partnership with Audible. I created four new audiobook titles in a matter of two years. None of that was even on my radar, and all of it was only made possible by chasing a dream I never achieved.

Keep going. Find your amazing ending.

Your life will take you to remarkable places if you believe in your abilities and encourage yourself to keep moving forward. Life is going to test you, but if you give up your timeline of *when* you'll achieve a dream, and you show up in that mirror every day, and maintain that high five attitude, you will eventually end up where you were meant to be. And if you don't achieve the goal you were working toward, it's because you weren't supposed to and life has something so much better in store for you. Something amazing. Believe that.

Your life is teaching you something. It always is. Everything, and I mean absolutely everything, is preparing you for what's coming next. That high five you give to the person in the mirror every morning is training yourself to trust that. Because if you are still breathing, there is still time. So keep going.

CHAPTER 13

Can I Actually Handle This?

Sometimes the you-know-what hits the fan. You weren't expecting it. You didn't deserve it. But now you're in it. Enter this thought on repeat:

Why is this happening to me? I can't handle this.

Then the red-hot monologue starts even before you get out of bed: *This feels too heavy and overwhelming . . . I never asked for this . . . If one more shoe drops, you'll need to check me into the 7th floor of Mass General . . . I just can't parent today . . . Turn off the news, I can't take it . . . I don't even know who I am anymore . . . I thought I followed all the rules and did everything right . . . Can I read that email from my kid's teacher without crying? . . . Oh God, how am I finding myself here again? Am I on the verge of a breakdown?*

It's times like these when your life turns upside down that you need to look—and I mean really look—at yourself in the mirror and say, "I know you're scared *and* I know you can do this." It is the kind of real talk and tender love you crave when you're afraid. Feeling fear is normal. It's what you do the moment after you feel the fear that makes a difference. You can be terrified of losing the game but still swing for the fences. You can be scared and still be confident in your ability to face this. You can feel the weight of the world on your shoulders and still stand tall.

So scared, I was split in two.

I'm sure you can remember exactly where you were when you realized that your life was about to change because of Covid. Maybe it was an email from work saying they were closing the office, or how eerily quiet your city got, or the nursing home where your grandmother lives closed the door to all its visitors, or you had screaming matches with your kids about coming home and quarantining. (Or maybe that was just me?)

Covid turned my life upside down on a Wednesday. I was taping my talk show in New York City when CBS called and said they found the virus in the building and we had to leave immediately. It all happened so fast that I never had a chance to say goodbye to the talk show team of 135 people that I had been working with for 10 months. Fire trucks were parked outside as I left the studio. Across 57th Street, the rest of our team was evacuating our office building, along with the staff from *60 Minutes, Last Week Tonight with John Oliver,* and *Entertainment Tonight.* As I jumped in the car and pulled onto the West Side Highway to head home to Boston, I thought, *What just happened?*

Moments of sudden change like this always draw a line in the sand. There is a before and after, and your life is never the same again. If you've ever faced a terrifying health scare, or had anyone you love die suddenly, or cheat on you, or you get fired from your dream job, or someone accuses you of something horrible that you didn't do, it splits your life into two parts. Your old life, or career, or relationship is gone, and the old you goes with it. Suddenly, you find yourself in unknown, brand-new territory. I've had all of these things happen during my lifetime, and when the pandemic hit, it felt just as discombobulating.

I wanted my old life back.

Change always offers a chance for growth if you choose to look at the challenging or painful experiences of your life that way. There's a quote I love: "The price of your new life is your old one." As much as I love that quote, and it's easy to post it on social media, that doesn't mean it's an easy concept to accept in real time. I'll be honest with you: as positive, confident, and optimistic as I am, when the shit hit the fan, I didn't want a new life—I wanted my old life back.

I had gone from feeling like I was on top of the world hosting a TV show to hitting a mental brick wall, in a matter of a few minutes. That's how fast you can go from high to low. The pandemic did that to everyone in the beginning, because it triggered fear in all of us. Fear of dying, of losing our jobs, of being alone, and of losing loved ones.

For me it also triggered all the old fears of my recent past and being in a financial free fall again. First, the show was canceled (which basically means I was fired), and then the rest of my business started to implode. Every speech I had booked for the year disappeared one by one. Then, I got fired again when my publisher canceled the contract for this book you are holding, meaning I had to return the advance they had sent me—money that was long gone.

I needed a high five.

When old fears get triggered, you start repeating old patterns instinctively. I felt stuck and powerless. The anxiety came rushing back in and I reached for the booze to numb my mind and I harped on my husband (*because obviously he's to blame for a global pandemic*).

What I needed during this time was encouragement. I needed someone to tell me I would be okay. I needed to be told the truth: I had faced challenges before, and this challenge wouldn't be easy, but I would be okay, and facing it would make me a better version of myself and my life more meaningful.

But at 51, I didn't feel like reinventing myself yet again. It pissed me off. Do you know how many times I had already reinvented my life? I'm sure you can relate to that on some level too. You didn't ask for the divorce, the car accident, the recession, the death in your family, the diagnosis, the unexpected bill. And you sure as hell didn't ask for the pandemic.

Every morning I woke up with a tremendous sense of dread. My stomach was hollow, my heart was pounding, and a wave of anxiety started in my ankles and would roll right up to my chest. By the time I woke up, I was in the grip of it.

In the past, I couldn't just lie in bed and stare at the ceiling. There were always reasons I needed to get out of bed. I had somewhere I needed to go, or someone who needed me.

The pandemic was different. There was nothing to do. No office to drive to. No plane to catch. No classes for my kids to attend. No coffee shop open to meet a friend at. No errands to run. No gym open. Nowhere I could escape to. It was just me and all the uncomfortable feelings in my body.

In the past, I've always soothed myself in one of two ways: launch myself into my day, or turn over and reach for Chris. His presence would make me feel secure. During the pandemic, I would wake up consumed with worry about all the uncertainty. Chris, on the other hand, was thriving during the pause that the pandemic created in all of our lives. Instead of worrying about things beyond his control, he doubled down on the habits that make him feel grounded and fulfilled. He was out of bed early, putting himself first and meditating, hiking, and journaling. He was doing what we all need to do: he was taking care of his deepest emotional needs.

So when I woke up in a panic, my two coping mechanisms were gone. With nowhere to run to and no one to cling to, I was forced to figure out how to help myself. So I lay in bed and just quietly told myself what I would have wanted Chris to tell me.

I high fived my heart.

Here's what this looks like: take a deep breath, close your eyes, put your hands on your heart, and tell yourself, "I'm okay. I'm safe. I'm loved."

Some mornings I would lie under the covers and repeat these three sentences to myself over and over again. And somehow, this soothing mantra calmed my nerves, quieted my anxiety, and settled my stress. Even though we were in a global pandemic, the news was terrifying, the racial injustice traumatizing, and no one knew if this would be a few days or a two-year-long ordeal—in that moment what I was saying was true: I was okay. I was safe. And I was loved.

Current Limiting Belief: *I can't handle this.*

Flip It: *I'm okay. I'm safe. I'm loved.*

How to feel comfortable in your own skin.

Tomorrow morning, try it. When you wake up, put your hand on your heart. Take a deep breath and say: "I'm okay. I'm safe. I'm loved." Repeat it as many times as you need. Feel the relief that flows into your heart and mind. You'll feel your body settle—you'll feel more connected to yourself, and you'll feel okay, safe, and loved—even the first time you use it.

You may need to say it a dozen times, or a hundred times. You may need to exhale deeply as you do. Say it as many times as you need. This habit will infuse you with a sense of peace and surety. And every morning as you continue to practice it, you will soothe your weary nervous system, retraining it to settle, and to relax. You're literally teaching your body what it feels like to be safe.

On bad mornings, when you feel your heart racing and you're filled with dread, repeating, "I'm okay. I'm safe. I'm loved" will interrupt your negative thoughts for a moment. Keep repeating it until you squash that downward spiral. As you feel yourself settle, you have an opportunity to lift your spirit, by focusing on something positive. If you don't know what to say, refer back to Chapter 7 and pick your favorite mantra.

Talk to yourself.

If you want to take this habit one step further, you can say your name as well: "Mel, you're okay. Mel, you're safe. Mel, you're loved." This takes things a level deeper for two reasons: First, because your RAS always hears your name, it alerts your brain that this soothing mantra is something to pay attention to.

Second, you can almost separate the voice that's talking to you from yourself. When I say, "Mel, you're okay," I find it especially comforting at a deeper level because it feels like another human being is telling me I'm going to be safe, okay, and loved. It's like seeing yourself in the mirror and realizing you are not alone. You have YOU!

When you talk to yourself in the third person, you leverage a concept in psychology called "the power of objectivity." Referring to yourself from a more objective perspective (aka using your own name or seeing your reflection) makes you better able to deal with negative emotions, even in highly charged situations.

Feelings are just waves. They come and go.

This habit teaches you how to surf the waves of emotion that can hit you, rather than letting them knock you over. I realize now what I was doing wrong all those years. I used to wake up and as soon as I felt that wave of worry and anxiety, I'd resist it. I'd react. I'd HATE that it was there.

I would go to bed every night dreading the thought that I'd wake up and feel it again. Guess what I was doing? I was teaching my mind and body to bring it on. I was putting so much energy into resisting and hating it that I was focusing on it and making it important! I was basically teaching my RAS and my nervous system to continue waking up in that miserable state. By using this tool, I take control. Sure, I still sometimes wake up and feel on edge, but I no longer dread it, because I know exactly what to do to quiet that feeling.

On the mornings when you wake up and feel awesome, you should still put your hands on your heart because you'll love how it feels. It feels like your favorite person just gave you a hug. It amps up your life force. You don't have to just use it when you wake up. Use it anytime you feel a wave and need some reassurance. Yesterday I used this tool when I felt a wave of anxiety hit me while I was at the grocery store.

Want to hear a crazy story?

The photographer who shot the photo of me on the back of this book, Jenny Moloney, just texted me as I was doing the final proofread of this manuscript. She was flying to LA and 15 minutes into the flight, the cabin pressure failed, they started descending fast, and the flight attendant ran up the aisle from the back of the plane telling everyone to put their seat belts back on. As they circled back to Boston, they practiced bracing for an emergency landing (you put your head down at your knees). They landed safely but with the wheels on fire (!!) to a runway full of first responders. She said, "I've never been so terrified in my life, but you want to know what got me through the entire ordeal . . . and two hours later, back on another plane?"

> **thanks**
> **I used the mantra and hand**
> **on** 🖤

Those three words *I'm safe. I'm okay. I'm loved* are magic. Because as long as you are alive and can say those words to yourself—it is true. In the moment, you are safe. You are okay. And you are loved.

After seeing a video where I talked about using this mantra in the morning, a woman named Maria started high fiving her heart. Maria told me that due to a number of past traumas, she woke up every morning with anxiety, just like I was, and felt like "someone is mad at me."

She shared that she was amazed how even from the first morning of trying this, there was a major change in her day-to-day life. She said, "That feeling of anxiety when you wake up can be so consuming, and even when you go on with your day, that feeling is in your body. It's there all the time and always in the back of my head.

"It's amazing how something so simple—putting your hand on your heart and saying 'I'm okay, I'm safe, I'm loved'—can be life-changing. As soon as I started doing it, even from the first morning, that anxious feeling isn't there all day. I'll still have small moments of anxiety, but I'm no longer carrying it through the day anymore."

While I was writing this book and hearing so many similar stories from people like Maria, it dawned on me that one of the reasons I often wake up and feel anxious first thing in the morning is because of something terrible that happened to me when I was just a kid. I was molested by an older kid during a sleepover. In fact it occurred when I was fast asleep, and at my most vulnerable.

This is what I meant when I said earlier that "life got its hands on you." It gets its hands on all of us, in one way or another. Sometimes we bury the memory of it because it's too scary, too painful, too confusing, too humiliating to face. But even buried it's doing a number on your body, mind, and spirit.

My childhood trauma created a "trauma response" and recorded it in my nervous system. That means my adult body still remembers the feeling of waking up in the middle of the night when I was a kid, knowing that something bad was happening to me, but not knowing how to stop it or even how to react to it. That body memory still echoes throughout my nervous system, which is why, 40 years later, I wake up feeling dread, fear, panic, confusion, and shame.

As a grown woman, my first thought when I open my eyes in the morning is "something is wrong." That often translates to "I've done something wrong" or "someone is mad at me." And the downward spiral deepens. Remember how I described it as starting in my ankles and rolling up to my chest? That "feeling" is my childhood trauma being remembered by my adult body.

I can't change this with positive thinking. I can't heal trauma with thoughts alone. I need actions that change my default response and that clear this residue from my nervous system. The trauma I experienced is not my fault. And my subconscious reaction to it, even four decades later, is not my doing. But it IS my responsibility to clear it away. If I want a high five life, it means finding the courage to face it. And one of the things that has helped tremendously is this high five to my heart that I do every morning.

Let's look at the research.

There's a reason you need to start every morning, not only with a high five in the mirror, but also with one to your heart. Studies show that without first calming your anxiety and settling your nervous system, there is NO WAY you'll be able to change anything.

I learned this from Dr. Judy Willis, the neuroscientist I introduced you to in Chapter 2. If you're in a stressed-out state, your brain flips into survival mode. It won't let ANY new positive information into your higher brain, where you learn new skills and create new memories. Instead, all it wants you to see are the threats around you. That's why stress and anxiety in the morning can feel like a gravity blanket pinning you to your bed.

The only option that truly works is settling your body. Lying in bed and thinking about all the things that scare you just intensifies what you're already feeling, and mindlessly launching yourself into your day only makes you drag that anxiety with you.

The good news? Turning off your body's stress response is as simple as putting your hand on your heart and giving it a high five, which will slow your body down and turn on your body's "rest and relax" nervous system.

There are two words that explain why you can turn on this powerful, calm state anytime: vagus nerve.

The vagus nerve is the longest nerve in your body, connecting your brain to every other organ. It carries information about pain, touch, and temperature, and it even controls the muscles in your throat and your vocal cords. It also allows your brain to facilitate the release of dopamine, which is a feel-good hormone that puts you in a more relaxed, calm mood.

Activating your vagus nerve is easy. You can do it by high fiving your heart. You can also activate it through any of these practices:

- *Breathe deeply and slowly*

- *Take a walk outside (especially in nature)*

- *Meditate*

- *Hum or chant*

- *Gargle water*

- *Sing at the top of your lungs*

- *Take a warm bath or a cold shower*

The vagus nerve is the reason putting your hand on your heart and calming yourself down BEFORE you affirm that you're okay, safe, and loved is such an effective way to rewire your brain. Putting your hand on your heart tells your body that you're safe and not stressed, which allows your RAS to be receptive to these mantras. So your RAS realizes that feeling safe and okay is important to you.

And the more you tell yourself you're okay, you're safe, and you're loved, the faster you will wake up and feel that way. Changing the story you're telling yourself, paired with a high five to your heart, will activate the vagus nerve and help you retrain your body's response from feelings of uncertainty and anxiety to feeling confident in your own skin.

It changes YOU.

Now, you may be thinking, *Oh my God, Mel Robbins. We're talking about past trauma, and you just told me to put my hands on my heart. You. Are. A. Moron.*

It may sound offensive for me to tell you that putting your hands on your heart is going to change the circumstances of your life. It doesn't. That's not what I'm saying.

High fiving your heart changes YOU. And when YOU change, YOU can change the circumstances of your life. Once you learn how to put your body in a grounded, calm state, you can do the work to heal past trauma.

If you think you may be dealing with trauma in your body, I also recommend that you learn as much as you can and get into therapy. You deserve to be supported in your healing journey to being whole and complete. There are lots of therapeutic modalities that are effective with healing trauma and helping you regulate your nervous system, including Eye Movement Desensitization and Reprocessing (EMDR) and new psychedelic guided therapies that are in clinical trials awaiting approval from the FDA and are showing tremendous results. I've done both and they've been life changing.

Everything I share is backed by powerful research. They are simple secrets that have profound results. So if you find yourself resisting, and not wanting to look in the mirror and give your reflection a high five, or put your hands on your heart to slow your body down, that's a sign that you really need it.

True confidence is telling yourself that you are okay, safe, and loved—and believing that it's true with every fiber of your being. When you do, you will come to realize that the one person in your life you can trust, no matter what is happening in the world, or in your family, or at your job, or in your classroom, is YOU. You can help yourself heal from past trauma. You can calm your body and reset your mind and set your spirit free to soar. It is the very definition of empowerment. It means you know you can wake up every day, have your own back, and handle anything that might come your way.

CHAPTER 14

Okay, You May Not Want to Read This Chapter

I wanted to call this chapter "How to Manifest Confidence," but I figured if you saw the word *manifest* in the title of this chapter, you might think:

Oh boy. Mel's about to get metaphysical. She's going to pull some Harry Potter magic right now. She's laying out her crystals, pulling tarot cards, and I bet she'll say the word miracle *within the first five sentences.*

You're kinda right.

I'm bringing it to the next level, but not with incense, abundance prayers, or a magic wand. You know I'm all about science and don't worry, this chapter is based on research, but it does go into the land of woo-woo. When you get good at controlling your RAS and cheering yourself forward, you can do crazy attracting-magical-miracle stuff (there's that word!) with these tools.

This isn't for the faint of heart, but if you want to make inspiring changes in your life that will give you goose bumps, I've got some stuff to tell you about the power of belief. I want you to encourage yourself to continue believing in the impossible. I know when I started doing that, my life got unbelievably better, and I'll share a story that will make you understand why belief is so important. As for the science, we'll get deep into the research of visualizing properly, so you can get your RAS running like a well-oiled machine to help you get what seems impossible right now.

What I'm about to prove to you is that your mind will conspire to help you get what you want. You just have to be willing to believe it.

I have a story to tell you about a painting.

It was my senior year of college and my parents were in town. That night, we got dressed up and drove to a famous Vermont glassblowing studio called The Mill at Simon Pearce, with a wonderful restaurant inside. As we walked into the building, my mind was fixated on cheddar cheese soup. My roommate told me I should order it because it was "unbelievable." When I walked into the restaurant that night, I saw, hanging on the wall, a large landscape painting. I didn't just notice the painting and walk on. I stopped dead in my tracks to stare at it. It was the size of a doorway, only turned on its side. Something about it seemed familiar and drew me in.

As I walked toward it, the noise in the restaurant seemed to disappear. Everything around me was suddenly quiet and still. I moved closer to the painting, and suddenly, strangely, it seemed that I'd stepped inside it. I realized it was a painting of a Vermont landscape. There was a broad, pale field in the painting. There were tall grasses and a stand of trees lined up in the middle of the field, growing smaller and smaller against the rising mountains, and a bright-blue cloudy Vermont sky. I could almost feel the breeze. I could smell the sweetness of fresh-cut hay. I could hear the geese announcing their arrival as they flew in formation above. I was no longer in the restaurant. I was standing in that field. All five of my senses were on fire. My mind, body, and spirit were perfectly attuned and focused on one thing—that painting.

More than just excitement, there was a desire, a knowing, a connectedness to something greater that I can't explain. I had never wanted to buy a piece of art before, but in this moment, I wanted to own that painting. Think about a moment in your life when an unexplainable wave of desire hit you like this. You just *knew* something, or someplace, or someone was meant for you. Your senses came alive, your mind focused, and your heart expanded. You were fully present in the moment. You were in your power. That is high five energy.

I would have that same feeling a few years later when I met my husband, Chris, for the very first time. I was ordering a bourbon on the rocks at a bar in New York City and I heard someone behind me say, "That sounds great, make it two." I turned around. There he was. The music and the noise in the bar disappeared and we just started talking, as if we had known one another for a thousand years. He asked me to marry him three days later.

A few years after that, I'd feel that same wave of desire again when we drove past an abandoned farmhouse outside of Boston. I told Chris to stop the car. The windows on the house were broken. The lawn was about a foot high. It didn't look like anyone but ghosts lived in it. I can't explain it, but all I wanted to do was buy that house. We were able to track down the deed in probate court. It never came on the market. We bought it from the estate of its dead owner and raised our family in it for the past 24 years.

These are examples of moments in my life when my thinking wasn't blocked. My mind was open. I knew what I wanted, and for whatever reason, I gave myself permission to believe I could have these things. That permission to believe you are capable and worthy of having what you desire is powerful. Your RAS takes note and immediately goes to work and adjusts the filter in your mind to help you achieve it.

Someday, it shall be.

I don't know how long I stood there staring at the painting. What I do know is that at some point, a waiter dropped a tray and sent a bunch of glasses shattering across the floor. It snapped me back into my body like a rubber band. And that's when it happened. From somewhere deep inside, I heard myself say it:

Someday I will own this painting.

I leaned forward to look at the price. $3,000.

Not today.

I exhaled and slowly backed away from it. The noise and energy of the bustling restaurant closed in, but my mind remained open. I thought, *I'll be back,* and turned to walk to the table where my parents had sat down. My mom asked me where I had been, and I said, "I was looking at that painting over there." My mom looked up in the direction of the painting and then looked back down at her menu.

This is a very important point about your desires. They are deeply personal. What's meant for you isn't meant for someone else. The things that draw you in are for you. That's why it's YOUR responsibility to do the work to go get them! Once you lock on to something, it stays with you like the entries in a diary that has been put on a shelf for safekeeping. It's filed away in your subconscious, just waiting for the moment when you think of it again.

How do you know if something is *not* meant for you? You'll feel the opposite energy. You won't be pulled toward it; you'll feel yourself push away from it. You'll feel like something inside you is shrinking.

If you wouldn't high five it, it's not yours.

Before I graduated that spring, I borrowed a friend's car and went to the restaurant one more time. I wanted to see the painting again. If you could fall in love with an object, I had. I wouldn't say I was obsessed. It was more like a possibility had opened up in my mind and I had unfinished business. Nicholas Sparks hadn't written any of his romance novels yet, but this could have been a scene out of one of them.

In less than a month, I would be leaving to start my new life after college. I sat at a table in the restaurant and had lunch just a few feet away from where the painting hung. I imagined hanging it in my own kitchen someday. That painting would be mine. I was just as sure of that fact as I was sure that I had just finished eating a bowl of cheddar cheese soup.

When I look back on the 21-year-old me eating lunch next to some painting I couldn't afford, it makes absolutely no sense. It's not like I was studying art or was a painter myself. I was a broke college student. Even if I did have $3,000, I sure as hell wouldn't have spent it on a painting. My parents would have killed me. Plus, I had nowhere to hang a painting that size. I was about to start my new life by following my boyfriend to Washington, D.C. I didn't even have a job yet.

I can't explain to you why this happened to me. I like to think it happened because I was supposed to tell you this story in this book, and the painting is evidence of the miracles you can create when you give yourself permission to want what you value and desire. It's so easy to imagine how this story ends if my mindset was blocked by negative thoughts. I would have told myself something negative: *You can't afford this. This is a waste of time. What the f*ck are you doing here?* Those negative thoughts would have triggered negative action. I never would have gone back to the restaurant.

The Zeigarnik effect.

Here's the interesting thing. Remember what you learned about the RAS? Telling your mind that something is important to you is like giving it a set of directives. That's also why you never forget the things you dream about. Your mind won't allow it. The secret is remaining open to the possibility that you are capable of making it happen.

There is no doubt that the experience flipped a switch in my mind. I left the restaurant with a silent resolve. There was this quiet certainty in my spirit. I was inspired, and that intention fueled my confidence. I knew in my bones that *someday I would own that painting*—and that is the only thought I would allow my mind to consider.

And sure enough, I didn't forget it. This is the mental coding I've been telling you about—it's called the Zeigarnik effect, which I mentioned in Chapter 10. When you are intentional about visualizing something that's important to you, your brain takes note and adds it to a mental checklist labeled "This Is Important" and stores it in your subconscious—don't you love that?

This means that your dream or goal is always in the background as "unfinished business," and your mind will look for every chance it gets to remind you of it. The RAS will scan the world and place reminders in your conscious mind.

That's why even when you say "It's too late," your goals and dreams haunt you. It's why Eduardo will always think about California. Why I will always think of being a *New York Times* Bestseller. It's why you see red Acuras when you want one. You may want to forget, but thanks to the Zeigarnik effect, your mind won't forget it. When it comes to your dreams, you have two choices: pursue them or be haunted by them.

I experienced the Zeigarnik effect all the time. If someone said the word *Vermont* or I saw a piece of hand blown glassware, the RAS let that information into my conscious mind. And, when I thought about the painting, I then thought about all the steps I'd take to make owning it happen.

I saw myself working hard, growing older, and putting small amounts of money aside to save for it. I saw the envelope of cash in my desk drawer. I imagined the wave of excitement and felt the grip of the handshake with the previous owner when I finally bought it. I could even feel the smile spread across my face, the kind that makes your cheeks tighten up, when it was mine. I saw a hook getting hammered into a wall. I could feel how heavy and awkward it was to hoist such a large work of art up and steady it as someone helped me lift it and place it on the wall.

Manifesting done right.

I didn't know it, but I was using visualization to bring that painting closer to me. There is some powerful science behind how manifesting confidence and visualization can change your RAS, but only when you do it right. Luckily, I was doing it the right way when I imagined the small steps I would take to get this painting. Let me explain.

Most people get manifesting wrong because they try to visualize and conjure the end result: winning the ski race or the Oscar, losing 50 pounds or having a million dollars in the bank. Manifesting done wrong can keep you stuck, because while big dreams are amazing, and you need to have them, manifesting the end result will NOT help you achieve them. Manifesting done *right* will help you make your dreams come true—or at least help you do the work.

Neuroscience research has shown that visualization makes it easier to work on your goals and dreams because it changes your RAS to spot opportunities that match that picture you just created in your head. But research out of UCLA shows us that in order to make visualization *really* help you achieve your goals, you need to *visualize yourself doing the hard, annoying, small steps along the way to reaching your dreams.*

That's because brain scans have shown that we stimulate the same brain regions when we visualize ourselves performing an action as when we actually perform that same action. So, you can mentally rehearse your future behaviors. Visualizing an action leads to you being more likely to follow through on that action. Remember, it's our actions that get results. Manifesting confidence means you have to envision yourself doing all the small, annoying steps along the way, not just basking in the blaze of victory at the finish line.

This is about getting your nervous system and your mind's filter ready to take action. When you visualize the actions you need to take, you socialize your mind and body to those feelings, and you tell your RAS, *Hard work is important.*

Visualize yourself running in the rain.

Here's how it works:

If you want to manifest a big dream of running the Boston Marathon, yes, write that dream down every day. To achieve it, however, don't visualize yourself crossing the finish line and the roaring applause of the crowd. Visualize yourself lacing up your running shoes when it's 10 degrees out. Close your eyes, and picture what it's going to feel like to be out there running mile 13 on your own because your earbuds just ran out of batteries. Feel in your body the sensation of your alarm going off at 5 A.M., and you're exhausted, and you look out the window and see it's pouring—and you start running in the rain.

If your dream is to run a business that brings in six figures a month, don't visualize the money hitting your account. Visualize what it feels like to be writing a blog post, exhausted, at midnight, after the kids are asleep. Close your eyes and feel, with every fiber of your being, hanging up the phone after being told NO on yet another sales call. Then see yourself pick up the phone and dial the next number.

If your dream is to have a loving, healthy relationship beyond what you've ever known, you'd better visualize yourself making that dating profile and going on some bad dates. Visualize how it feels to be in therapy, doing the hard work to heal yourself and get rid of the codependent patterns that led you into bad relationships in the past.

THAT is how you make those massive, incredible dreams of yours come true. When the moment comes, your whole being is ready for it. When the day of your 13-mile training run shows up, and it's 5 A.M. and 10 degrees, and you are staring at yourself in the bathroom mirror—you won't talk yourself out of it. Because you've already visualized and socialized your mind to this moment, you'll raise your hand to your reflection and be ready: *13 miles. 10 degrees. I can do this. Let's go!*

If you want to manifest a painting? You do exactly what I did. Picture yourself working hard to make the money to buy it. Saving money each month. Buying a frame. The little things along the way. In my case, I was encoding the possibility into my mind by thinking about it and allowing myself to imagine what those steps would feel like as I took them.

This is just the beginning of a story that spans a decade.

As the years passed, the painting faded further into the background of my subconscious mind, and life took over. I moved to Washington, D.C., after college and started working, and then on to Boston to attend law school. And finally on to New York City, where I met my husband, Chris, and started practicing law. We got married, moved back to Boston for Chris's job, and began our life together. At this stage in my life, years passed by, and when Chris suggested we plan a weekend trip to Vermont to see the fall foliage, that painting was all I could think about. I told Chris the story of seeing it almost a decade before, and I insisted we plan the trip so we could stop by The Mill for lunch and see if it was still there.

The trip was weeks away, but the mere thought of seeing the painting again—not buying it, just seeing it—energized my spirit and inspired my mind to start dreaming bigger again. Now the painting moved from the back of my mind where it was stored, working its magic and trying to find its way to me, to the front of my mind, like a spotlight. Thank you, RAS! What an exhilarating feeling. I know you know what I mean. We've all had this feeling, the anticipation of something we want edging closer and closer to us. It feels like a celebration of the spirit, even before we get it ... even if we never do.

As we drove, I could feel that energy moving through my body like electricity traveling through a cord to light up a lamp. The closer we got, the clearer the painting appeared in my mind. Pulling up to The Mill, all five senses were on fire. As we walked in, hanging in the entrance was another painting by the same artist, Gaal Shepherd. My heart leapt. *It's a sign. Oh my God, it's still here.* I grabbed Chris's hand and led him through The Mill, room by room, frantically looking for my painting.

It was gone.

Chris put his arm around me. "I'm so sorry, honey."

The most surprising thing about that moment was the fact that Chris was more disappointed than I was. I was a little sad, but I think I would have been more surprised if it was still there after all these years. And here's the most important takeaway: a high five attitude believes anything is possible, even when it seems all hope is lost.

I looked up at him and I said, "It's okay. We can't afford to buy it anyway. This is now a quest." Then I laughed and added, "It'll probably take me forty years to be able to afford it, and I'll have to track down the estate of whoever bought it, because the original owner will be dead. But I'm going to find that painting." I believed I would.

Life went on, and that painting got filed away in my subconscious mind again. We bought a fixer-upper. I got pregnant with our first child. And then one year, for my birthday, Chris asked our friends and family to all chip in so I could get something nice for our new home. He handed me a card with several hundred dollars in it and told me to buy anything I wanted. I'm sure he thought I was going to get something practical, like a few stools for our kitchen.

But the painting was all I could think about. Now, keep in mind, a few hundred dollars wasn't going to buy me anything by this artist. And certainly not "my painting." The artist had grown very popular over the previous decade and was shown in art galleries around the United States. But an open mind just lets that negative garbage pass through the filter. And in my mind, money plus the permission to get "anything I wanted" meant opportunity. When your mind is open, that's what it will see: opportunities everywhere. That's your RAS and the Zeigarnik effect helping you.

I didn't stop and think about the list of reasons this would never happen. I didn't talk myself out of this like I did other things. Doubt wasn't pumping through my veins; inspiration was. I picked up the phone as if I had a million dollars burning a hole in my pocket and called The Mill. A nice man came to the phone, and I explained the situation. He said he would be happy to send me a few Polaroids of the artist's "small pieces."

When he said "small pieces," I felt my cheeks get red. And I felt my nervous system go hot. As soon as your body goes into an alarm mode, your RAS will lose its focus and negative thoughts will flood. This is how quickly you go from high to low.

What on earth am I doing? I mean, who am I to buy a piece of art? Our furniture is a mix of hand-me-downs and things from Ikea. And the closest thing I own to "art" is the Matisse poster on our fridge that was in my college dorm room. And small pieces? Shit, I can't even afford one of her small pieces. I'm a pregnant 30-something who's just making the ends meet. I should hang up right now.

I was embarrassed that I didn't have a lot of money. And I was starting to think maybe I should use the money to buy something we needed, like a crib for the baby we were about to have.

I could feel my mind starting to close off. The stress in my body triggered a negative reaction in my mind. The second that guy said "small pieces," the negative thoughts that hit my brain started stirring like a dust cloud. And when you feel the dust storm of lint brewing in your mind, you have to wipe it away. Because, like I've said, when your thoughts are negative, you'll take negative action, which is why I almost hung up the phone.

When you feel your nervous system go hot and flood with stress, you have to intervene. Remember how Dr. Willis said when your body is stressed it impairs your cognitive ability? This is that moment! To help you, the 5 Second Rule works like a charm. Just count 5-4-3-2-1 and it will interrupt the downward spiral. Unfortunately, I hadn't invented the Rule yet. So I did the next best thing: I took a deep breath, I thought about the painting, and I said, "I'm not thinking about that," and I visualized that painting hanging in my kitchen, and summoned that high five energy.

I said to him, "By the way, there was this one piece that I absolutely loved. It was there for years and years. It's about the size of a door turned on its side . . ." and I went on to describe the painting of the Vermont landscape in great detail.

He paused, and said, "Well, I've only been here for a little more than a year, and her pieces come in and out of here pretty quickly. I would hate to take a guess because I think it was gone by the time I started working here. But you know what . . . Gaal would probably know."

"Gaal? You mean the artist, Gaal Shepherd? You know Gaal?"

He laughed. "Of course I know Gaal. She lives a few miles from here. Let me go get her number."

I almost had a heart attack.

I'd had a secret connection with this woman for more than a decade, and now I had her phone number. What on earth would I say to her, especially knowing I couldn't actually afford to buy one of her paintings, even, as the guy said, "a small piece"?

Notice that I'm starting to feel stressed again, which opens the door to negative thoughts. If you get stressed, your mind loses its ability to stay positive and open. You cannot allow your mind to close like that because negative thoughts lead to negative action. I started procrastinating. For a few days, I paced around the apartment, trying to think of the perfect thing to say.

Chris kept asking me, "Did you call her yet?"

I had endless excuses for why I hadn't made the call. The truth is, I was scared. I felt self-conscious. I wanted her to like me. I was scared of saying something stupid and making a fool of myself. I wasn't a sophisticated art buyer, and I was sure that's the kind of person she was used to dealing with. People pleasing was paralyzing me.

Finally, Chris had had enough. He handed me the phone and said, "Mel, if you don't call her right now, I'm going to start dialing." He had that frustrated look on his face that meant he was serious.

"Okay, I'll do it."

The phone rang a few times, and then she picked up. She had barely said, "Hello," and I was already talking a mile a minute. Luckily, I didn't scare her and I didn't make a fool of myself. It was the opposite. We connected immediately. At one point she asked me why I was so fond of her work. The answer was effortless. I told her that Chris and I spend a lot of time hiking in the mountains and that "I've had these moments where I come around a bend and there is a view that takes my breath away. I've often wondered in those moments if anybody else sees what I see, and your work confirms that someone else does."

And then I said what I had really wanted to say all along: "By the way, there was this one piece that I absolutely loved. It was there for years and years. It's about the size of a door laid on its side . . ." and I went on to describe the painting in great detail. There was silence. I could hear her thinking.

And then she said, "You know, Mel, over the years, I've painted hundreds of large-format Vermont landscapes and I would hate to mistake which one you're referring to. So how about this? How about you and Chris pick a date? You come up to The Mill and my husband and I will meet you and we'll all walk around. I'll tell you the stories behind every painting that's hanging there. And if you don't like anything that you see, we can go back to my studio, which is a couple of miles away, and I can show you everything that I'm working on. And if nothing connects with you there, you can look through my slides and maybe you'll be able to find a slide of that painting."

A month later we headed up to meet Gaal and her husband for lunch. She was lovely, about twice our age, and they greeted us like old friends. We walked all around The Mill, looking at her work as she told us the story behind each piece. People were coming up to her and saying hello, and my excitement was slowly starting to turn to dread because I realized we couldn't afford any of the paintings we were looking at. Eventually we sat down for lunch in that same restaurant where I had first seen the painting in 1989. And, yes, I got the cheddar cheese soup.

After we ordered, Gaal looked at me and said a sentence I will never forget, "Now that you're sitting down, I have something to tell you." The noise in the busy restaurant seemed to disappear.

And she continued. "I've never experienced anything like what I am about to tell you. When you called me and described the painting to me on the phone, I pretended that I didn't know what you were talking about. Mel, I knew exactly what painting you meant."

Her husband interrupted. "You should have seen her when she hung up the phone with you—she looked like she had seen a ghost."

Gaal nodded and then said, "There have only been two times in my entire career as an artist that I've done two versions of the same scene, at the same time. Your painting is one of a pair. I gave one of the paintings to The Mill to sell and I put the other one in storage in my studio."

And then she started tearing up as she said, "The sister painting to the one that you saw in this restaurant all those years ago is still in my studio a few miles from here. I've never taken it out of storage. It's just been sitting there all these years. That's why I froze the moment you started describing your painting on the phone. You were describing the painting that was in storage. I had thought about getting it framed and selling it a dozen times. Now I know why I never did. I guess it was waiting for you to come looking for it."

Something magical was happening.

We all knew it as we sat there in awe. After lunch we drove to her studio down the road. And as we walked in, right there in the center of the studio, was an easel. And on the easel was a large piece of plywood with the sister painting to mine taped against it.

It was the most exquisite moment of my life. It was as if time collapsed and I was living two moments, 11 years apart, at the exact same time. It felt like I was standing in that bustling restaurant all those years ago, declaring that this painting would be mine, and also, simultaneously, standing in the present moment with the painting. It was the most profound sense of intuition, knowing, and connectedness to something deeper that I have ever experienced. It's why I believe that this moment is preparing you for something that's coming.

I don't know how long I stood there in Gaal's studio looking at that painting. At some point, Chris put his arm around me, and my heart sank.

We couldn't afford to buy it.

I looked up at Chris, and he didn't skip a beat: "Hey, Gaal, how much for the big one?"

She replied, "Well, Mel can have that one for five hundred dollars. Because clearly when I created it, I was doing it for her."

My heart split open. It was one thing to see the painting. It was a whole other level to be able to purchase it. It was mine. I had done it. For 11 years, I gave myself permission to believe that I could have what I wanted. I fought off negative thoughts. I never lost my inspiration. I kept my mind open to the possibility. I kept walking down the path toward it. I believed it, and my mind helped me achieve it. I manifested what I wanted. I high fived myself forward every step of the way.

I felt exhilarated and exhausted at the same time. I've thought a lot about the exhausted part. It wasn't emotional exhaustion. It was mental. After 11 years of keeping this painting on my brain's "This Is Important" list, my mind could finally check the box and let it go. It had done its job. The painting could now live on a wall instead of hanging out in the back of my mind. It was a gigantic sense of accomplishment.

I walked out of her studio with the painting. When I brought it home, the only wall in our house that it could fit on was in our bedroom. I had to tack it up on the wall because it would take another year before I could afford to frame it.

The painting hangs in my kitchen today and you can see me standing in front of it if you flip to the "About the Author" page at the back of the book. It's evidence, a physical reminder, proving something I believe deeply:

Your mind is designed to help you achieve your dreams.

Your job is to believe it is possible and encourage yourself to keep walking toward it. No matter what, keep believing and give up your timeline for when and how it unfolds.

It took 11 years of believing before I owned that painting. And it turns out this story didn't stop with the painting. I now realize that the fact that my dream painting depicts a beautiful, inviting Vermont landscape is no coincidence. It was a mile marker leading me to a destination.

I think of it as a big, celestial arrow in the sky, pointing me toward the chapter I'm living in my life right now, two decades later. I'll tell you that story in the next chapter. You can always connect the dots in your life if you are looking back. The true art is believing that this moment right now is a dot that is connecting you to something amazing that's coming in the future.

Trust is a major component of that—trusting in yourself, your abilities, and in the divine nature of things. That everything in your life is preparing you for something that hasn't happened yet. You may not be able to see how all the dots connect on the map of your life, but they do indeed connect.

You might not fall in love with someone at the bar tonight, or hit the bestseller list this time, or win the election, or land the funding from that VC firm, or get into the master's program you wanted. The point isn't to get things *when* you want them. It's to allow those things that you want to pull you forward through your fears and doubt and resignation. Your dreams teach you how to believe in something greater. They teach you to believe in YOURSELF and your ability to make anything happen.

So trust that. Trust in yourself and your ability to rise to this challenge, cheer yourself forward, and take care of yourself along the way. And every morning, as you stand face-to-face with yourself, just take a moment to smile, knowing that at some point in this beautiful life of yours, it will all make perfect, even magical, sense. And as you raise your hand to your reflection, without uttering a word, say, "I believe in you . . . I love you. Now, keep going, because something amazing is coming."

CHAPTER 15

Eventually, It Will All Make Sense

Have you ever felt like something feels off in your life, but you just can't put your finger on it? That was me these past few years. It wasn't there all the time, but in moments of stillness, I felt restless.

Every time I was on a plane for work and took off and landed in a new city, I'd have this agitated moment of envy and curiosity, thinking about where Chris and I would settle next. Two of our three kids had left the nest, and somehow our awesome farmhouse didn't quite fit us anymore. But I was so busy either traveling for work or engaged with my family as the kids were getting older, that I never had time to sit quietly with myself. The only time I felt close to my own thoughts was when I was 30,000 feet in the air. As the plane I was on touched down on the runway, I'd think, *Here? Austin? San Diego? Nashville? New York City? Is this the next chapter for us?*

And then, right before the pandemic hit, our son Oakley—who was in eighth grade at the time and in the throes of figuring out where to go to high school—threw us a curveball. He started insisting that he wanted to go to high school in southern Vermont, where my husband's parents have lived for two decades. At this point we had lived outside Boston for almost 25 years. Our team was in Boston. Our friends were in Boston. Our life was in Boston. I love southern Vermont, but my reaction was a hard NO.

I believe my exact words were "Move to Vermont? That's where people go to retire." I could not fathom moving to "the middle of nowhere." I was not going to leave my friends or the life we built in Boston. I could not possibly compete in business unless I was in a big city. And commute from a regional airport, almost two hours away? No way!

But Oakley persisted. His dyslexia had made school a tough road for him, and he was certain, in his bones, that the right next step was this public high school in Vermont. I was certain he could find an awesome school in the Boston area. Chris and I fought about it. My mother-in-law was pushing the idea to Chris behind the scenes. She even tried reminding me how much Chris loves to ski, to which I said, "I don't care what Chris likes to do. There's no way I am moving to Vermont!"

Have you ever heard that saying "Life is what happens when you're busy making other plans"? Well, I was busy making plans NOT to move to Vermont. I guess I wasn't paying attention to where all of the dots were actually leading me.

A psychic medium connected the dots.

Yes, you read that right. A month after I told Oakley we were not moving, a psychic medium was a guest on my talk show. She had been able to see and communicate with dead people since she was five. *(I love this type of stuff.)* She gave a couple of mesmerizing readings to people in the audience that were so spot-on that she had us all in tears—and every skeptic in the audience and our control room was converted.

Then, she turned to me and asked if she could give me a reading. Of course I said yes.

She told me there was a man standing behind me and he was in a military uniform. I immediately thought of my deceased grandfather Frank Schneeberger, who had been in the navy, but she said no. This was a decorated pilot. He was in the air force. *Pilot?* I thought. There's no one I know who was a pilot in the air force.

She said, "Does the letter *K* or the name 'Ken' mean anything to you?"

I said, "Ken? That's what we call our daughter Kendall. She was named after Chris's dad. My father-in-law's name was Kenneth. We called him Ken, too, but he was never in the military. He ran an advertising agency."

The medium said, "Well, whoever is standing behind you is getting agitated, and he wants you to verify this information with your family." *(The nerve of dead people.)*

At this point the producers got Chris on the phone, and to my amazement, Chris confirmed that his father had in fact been in the air force reserves in college, something I never knew. He never got a chance to fly because the pilot's test revealed Ken was color-blind, but it had always been his dream.

The psychic nodded. She seemed to know Ken was just the kind of guy who would pick an obscure (and un-Google-able) detail like that to suspend all disbelief. She then proceeded to tell me that Ken had lots of grandkids (true), but the youngest, and one he had been keeping an eye on, was our son. And that Ken came here today to send me a message: "There's something brewing about a school, and you don't like it, Mel, but you must listen to your son."

I literally had an out-of-body experience. I could not feel the chair underneath me, because in that moment, I felt like I was floating. I could feel Ken's presence. I knew he was there.

Now, I had not told a soul about the fights I was having with Chris and Oakley about moving to Vermont. And I mean, no one.

As far as I was concerned, the decision had already been made. A month ago. Oakley was going to school in Boston.

I knew exactly what Ken was telling me: *Move to Vermont. Trust.*

The story gets even crazier.

I walked off the set mumbling to myself, "I can't believe this. I have to move to Vermont." I was in a state of shock because I knew that this message was the truth.

I called Chris and told him about what had just happened. Chris said back, "I didn't tell you this, but yesterday my mom called. A year ago she wrote to the owner of a condo in the development where a bunch of her friends live. The owner just wrote her back, and apparently she's just put her offer in. She called me yesterday to ask if we wanted to buy the house she and Dad built. I told her no, that we had made the decision to stay in Boston."

Everything fell quiet. I took a leap of faith and said, "Tell her yes. We'll buy the house."

So right before the pandemic hit, we bought the house my in-laws had built, and we are now in the process of renovating it. We enrolled Oakley in the public high school he'd picked out. And yes, Chris very happily skis every day. I can look out my kitchen window and see for 140 miles and never see another person (which on some days terrifies me). But something else happened too.

I started to realize that for the past five years as I was rushing through my hectic life, I had lost a connection to myself. And if I am being honest, to Chris and the kids. The only reason I began to see and feel it was because of the comparative calm of the Vermont countryside. It turned out to be a perfect backdrop to illuminate what was going on within me. I finally had no choice but to get quiet and still. To pull out that filter, examine the lint, and clean it out once and for all.

Moving to Vermont brought me up close to my fears around not being successful enough. I had insecurity and doubt that if I lived in a town of 3,000 people, which is the same size as the town I grew up in, I wouldn't be able to find friends or a team to help me expand my business. I would fall behind and not be able to keep up with everyone else in Boston, Los Angeles, or New York. All my fears and insecurities came rushing toward me. I came face-to-face with myself.

It also made me realize that I always regulated my anxiety and stress by trying to outrun it. If I was always on the go—racing to a meeting, running to Target, making another call—it couldn't catch up with me.

It's a miraculous thing when you find out who you really are.

When life says, *This is meant for you*, listen. Never in a million years would I have visualized Vermont as the place I would be right now. All I know is what I said I wanted. Less time spent traveling. More time with my family. Less time worrying, more time being certain about my work and the direction it's heading. Less anxiety, more joy. Be careful what you wish for, because your RAS is paying attention.

In the process of writing this next chapter, both in my life and in this book, I had to intentionally and deliberately downshift. I had to embrace what I've been saying I want all along. Getting off planes and getting off the road. Doing my work in my own way and living in a place of my own choosing that makes me feel more content and fulfilled. I'm serious about letting go of all those stories I've been telling myself about who I need to be and how I need to live in order to be successful. I feel as though I'm embarking on the most creative chapter of my entire life because I'm not so busy running around. It's exciting and terrifying. Just like life—a wave of highs and lows I'm choosing to ride.

And I realized I do have a team. My team is virtual, as so many teams are now. Except for one person, Jessie, who was a video producer for the Baltimore Ravens, but then her fiancé got a job with Orvis and suddenly she moved to Vermont, right before the pandemic struck. It just so happened that one of my most pressing needs was to find a video editor for my social media team. Here she is, like a gift. And then, another: a copywriter from outside New York, Amy, who arrived this fall like we did, drawn to the same school and the change of lifestyle this region provides. And another, Tracey, who has been one of my most valued colleagues, moved to Vermont, where her partner was starting medical school. All of us shipwrecked together in this new chapter.

Each day my RAS shifts from *What the hell have I done?* to *Will this work?* to *This is working* to *THIS is EXACTLY where I need to be.* And I also have confidence knowing that even though this new chapter is amazing, if it's ever time for something new, I have the tools to change my life again.

Waking up in Vermont has taught me the single biggest lesson of my life, and that is: you are your own beacon. Yes, I have said repeatedly that the purpose of your dreams is to act like a beacon and pull you through the challenging moments of your life. But remember: you were born with those dreams. They are woven into your DNA. They are a part of you, which means you are the light.

The mistake we all make is that we rely on something external to tee us up. The idea that you have to have the greatest love affair or the most lucrative job or the fanciest house: you think all those things will make you feel like life is high fiving you when, actually, the inverse is true. You have to learn how to do it for yourself. You have to create the feelings you want in your life—the feelings of happiness, joy, optimism, confidence, celebration. That feeling of being cheered for: it begins with you giving that to yourself.

I can tell you that I've never before experienced the level of pure contentment that I do now. I've certainly been a very positive person. I've had bursts of happiness and a lot of fun. But in terms of feeling connected to myself and grounded in a vision for my life—that's always eluded me, and I never knew why. And I also know I couldn't have moved here any sooner. Everything that came before has prepared me to be here now. Dots connecting on the map of my life and leading me where I'm meant to go. Just like the dots of your life are leading you to whatever is meant for you.

That doesn't mean it was easy or perfect.

Change never is. For the first four months we owned the house, every other day I would wake up and drive to Boston. (I'm not kidding.) Because that's what you do when you feel blocked and you can't handle it: you flee. I realize I've been doing this my whole life: running. I exude confidence, but for many years I was never truly comfortable in my own skin. Not when I was around other people, and most definitely not when I was experiencing major changes or uncertain situations. This change has taught me how to feel the waves of uncertainty and fear, and not run, but to stand firm and feel the discomfort, to look myself in the mirror, and reassure myself: I will be okay.

When I met my new primary care doctor, a Vermonter through and through, he told me that in 40 years, he's seen a lot of people relocate here and most don't like it. He said, "Everybody runs somewhere, and it's usually away from their problems. But you just bring your problems with you wherever you go. In a new environment, especially a quiet, calm one like this, you've got nowhere to run. You've got to just be with yourself."

What I realized is, like a caged bird beating its wings, I had to sit with my discomfort and listen to it. I had to wake up in the morning and put my hand on my heart and tell myself what I needed to hear. I had to look for hearts and trust that I could see other signs. I had to high five myself in the mirror and cheer myself through the fog and the negative thoughts and into the day.

I learned to trust every last tool
I have given you in this book.

And I want you to trust them too. Your life is teaching you something. It's preparing you for something amazing you can't see. The discomfort is temporary. You've got to 5-4-3-2-1, put one foot in front of the other. You have to keep your filter clear and your mind open. It's because of the High 5 Habit, I could see very clearly that yes, I can grow my business on the side of this mountain. I can build a team here. And there's enough room for a pool table in the barn. The painting can hang in my kitchen. Chris and I can be deeply happy here. No, we will be. Because that's what I want.

Dreams don't disappear. You were born with them, and they are meant for you. That means you take them with you wherever you go and in whatever version of yourself you create. So you might as well stop running and start leaning into them. You might as well *see* and *hear* and *feel* all the clues your life is giving you about who you are destined to be. We are called in different ways to be the best and highest versions of ourselves. We want a high five marriage, we want to be high five parents. We want high five friendships and a high five career. Wherever there's a dream in your life, trust that you can high five your way to it.

And know that I'm still right beside you, raising my hand in celebration with you. High five, my friend. I see you. I believe in you. Now, it's your turn to believe in yourself and go make your dreams come true.

Wait, Wait . . . There's More!

How to Wake Up for Yourself

You know I just can't stop there with me on a mountain, raising my hand in the air to high five you . . . Because I know what you're thinking:

Ok, Mel. You had me at "high five my mirror" . . . but I'm confused. Am I supposed to move to Vermont with you? Talk to a psychic medium? I'm not sure . . . Do I buy a painting? Do I need a prom dress? I'm looking for hearts and Acuras? Sounds like I'm flipping my RAS on it's A-S-S? What am I doing, exactly? Walk me through this because you promised in Chapter 1 to "hold my hand."

I'm glad you asked—I've got you covered! Let's go back to the very beginning, where we first met: your bathroom mirror, in your underwear, and incorporate all the tools and research you've learned in this book:

A high five morning.

A high five morning is a series of simple promises. Each promise is backed by research, super easy, feels good, and creates a series of small wins that send you into your day, ready to rock and roll.

It starts when your alarm rings. Below, you'll see both the action you're going to take, and the deeper thing it's teaching you to do.

Here's how it goes:

✓ *Put yourself first—Get up when the alarm rings.*

✓ *Tell yourself what you need to hear—Say, "I'm okay. I'm safe. I'm loved."*

✓ *Give yourself a gift—Make your bed.*

✓ *Celebrate yourself—High five the mirror.*

✓ *Take care of yourself—Put your exercise clothes on.*

✓ *Train your RAS—Dream in the morning.*

A high five morning is one where you come first. These promises help you prioritize yourself, your needs, and your goals before your to-do list, your phone, social media, emails from work, turmoil in the news, the needs of your family, and everything else outside your control. When you keep these simple promises to yourself, you come first. Every morning. Every day of your life. Period. Just like the high five, at first glance, the list seems kind of dumb and obvious, so I'm going to unpack each promise so you understand the deeper meaning behind each step.

#1: Put yourself first—Get up when the alarm rings.

At night, before you turn out the light, take a minute to think about tomorrow morning. *What kind of morning do you need in order to feel supported?* What time do you REALLY need to get up in order to have enough time for yourself? Often, we get up at the same time every day out of habit.

When you think about what you need at this moment in your life, you may have to get up earlier. You may have to go to bed earlier. If you've got little kids at home or an early day at work and you want to get 15 minutes of exercise and meditation in, that time might have to be 5:00 or 6:00 A.M. It is what it is. Drop the drama and set the alarm. You may have to bail on a few nights out with your friends to get the sleep you need. Put yourself first.

When the alarm rings, get up. No snooze button. No drama. 5-4-3-2-1, just get up. This has nothing to do with being a morning person. This is where the science that you're learning is really important. Your RAS is paying attention. If you always hit the snooze button, you are telling your RAS you do not do what you say you're going to do, and that impacts how the RAS filters your view of yourself.

This is more than a wake-up call. It's more than an alarm. It's a promise. When you set the alarm clock tonight, you are making a promise. You are saying I matter. Tomorrow, when the alarm goes off, keep that promise. Get up immediately. In the morning, don't hear the alarm as an obligation. Hear it as an opportunity. This is a signal that the next 10 to 30 minutes are a gift for you.

And this is important: Do. Not. Look. At. Your. Phone.

#2: Tell yourself what you need to hear— Say, "I'm okay. I'm safe. I'm loved."

Now, center yourself. Instead of starting your day transfixed by whatever appears on the screen of your phone, put your hand on your heart and say, "I'm okay. I'm safe. I'm loved" as many times as you need to hear it. Congratulations, you just racked up two small wins: you got up and you took care of your needs, and the sun isn't even up. High five—you did it! You centered yourself and put yourself first.

#3: Give yourself a gift—Make your bed.

I started making my bed so I wouldn't crawl back into it and bury myself under the covers when my life was imploding ten years ago. Over time I realized that making your bed is another way to strengthen the muscle of discipline and commitment. It's also a beautiful gift you can give to yourself. It's a gift because whenever you walk into your bedroom today, you will see a beautiful bed rather than a mess you need to fix. Plus, when you come into your bedroom tonight, you've created a beautiful spot to lay down and dream.

You're making your bed for YOU. You're making your bed because you said you would. I do it every single morning, no matter where I'm staying. I even make my half of the bed if Chris is still sleeping. Why? Because the key to putting yourself first is practicing what you said you needed to do ahead of any excuse, feeling, or change in location.

#4: Celebrate yourself—High five the mirror.

Head straight to the bathroom and say hello to your biggest ally and best friend—YOU. Smile. Raise your hand in celebration. Take a moment for yourself. You got this!

#5: Take care of yourself—Put your exercise clothes on.

I move my body every day. The physical and mental benefits are backed by science and real-life evidence. You know it as well as I do: you've gotta move and break a sweat. But knowing this is not enough to make you do it. Even though you're well aware that you should move your body every day, it's the last thing you probably want to do.

So I devised a simple habit: I lay out my exercise clothes every night, like a trap on the floor of my closet, and doing this forces me to put them on in the morning before I leave my bedroom. If I were to step over them, I'd basically be saying, "F-off, Mel," so I'm guilting myself into doing it (productive guilt). Once those yoga tights are on and you're already dressed for it, it's a lot easier to remember to do it.

That's why I don't frame this promise as *"Work out every day."* That feels too hard. And if you already feel overwhelmed by your life, you won't be able to keep that promise. I want the bar for wins to be LOW. I want you to build momentum. You get a high five just for pulling those darn tights on. That's how I roll. Celebrate all the things! That's why I keep the promises easy: Hands on heart. Get up. Make your bed. High five the mirror. Put on the exercise clothes. Boom! Five wins and you haven't even had coffee yet!

You're now one step closer to the ultimate goal, which is to move your body. I'm making this easy because the whole point of waking up for yourself is to do it.

#6: Train your RAS—Dream in the morning.

When you think of dreaming, you usually think of sleeping. I want you to start dreaming in the morning as a way to bring your dreams into your day-to-day life.

Here's how: I sit down with my *High 5 Daily Journal* and do a two-page journaling practice every single morning. If you're interested in trying it out, I've put free templates for this journaling method and a little explanation of the science behind it as a gift to you at the end of this section.

At the top of the first page, I check off all the things I just did to center myself and wake up for myself. Checking those boxes reinforces the feeling of achieving each small win. It's a simple way to celebrate the progress you're making and the discipline you're building. It takes less than a minute and by the time I'm done, I'm feeling really present and proud.

Next, there's a spot to clear your mind. Doing a "brain dump" is a great way to wipe the filter in your mind clean. Just write exactly what you're feeling. Some days it'll be beautiful. Other days, it's word vomit. But on all days, it gets you out of your head and into the present moment with yourself. It helps you process any emotions, good or bad, and get them onto paper. I find that when I don't do that in the morning, I tend to expel those buried feelings and subconscious thoughts onto my family, my colleagues, and the poor dog. (Sorry guys.)

Then I give myself permission to get in touch with what I WANT. Just write five things that you want. Don't judge them, or smirk at them, or change them. Just write whatever your heart says to write.

It could be that you hope a loved one who is struggling with depression will feel like himself again. I recently wrote that I dream of selling out a two-day transformational event for 5,000 people and building a beach house at an amazing spot we love in Rhode Island. Sometimes I write about just being able to swim in the ocean and enjoy myself without thinking about being attacked by a shark. Some mornings your desires might be about money, taking a trip with your mom, or buying a tricked-out new Bronco truck. Whatever it is, give yourself permission to want it, and writing it down fires up that RAS to help you get it.

They can be the same ones every day, or they can be different. They can be your deepest, wildest, biggest dreams or just something you feel in your heart. It could be something you want to buy.

Or a way you want to feel. Or just something you want to do. Give yourself permission to dream with the lid off. Do it without apology. You validate your dreams by writing them down. The old you said no so many times to your dreams. Train your RAS to say YES.

This is a high five morning. Now that you've put yourself first and focused your RAS on what you want, feel free to look at your phone (or look for hearts) as you choose.

I can't WAIT for you to do this.

These practices are simple. But I want you to trust that doing them, one after the other, every morning doesn't just set you up for a better and more productive day. These practices are far more extensive. They will quiet your nervous system, focus your mind, and support you.

A high five morning is about building confidence. In yourself. In your body. In your thoughts. And in your spirit. These promises help set you up for success, create an intention for your day, and give you a sense of control before you step out into the world—which only makes you feel more confident.

And by dreaming in the morning, those wants, desires, and intentions go from the back of your mind to the front of it. They begin to walk beside you. You begin to know in your heart and soul that each and every day, you wake up, celebrate yourself, and are cheering yourself toward the thing you want—that we all want. The one thing we all wish for those we love dearly and deeply. That thing you need to envision and create for yourself:

A high five life.

A Gift from Mel

Don't ever accuse me of not giving you something. I told you that I have a special journaling practice. And now I'm sharing it with you . . . for FREE!

THE

High 5

DAILY JOURNAL

That's right, I want you to download the free templates or get your own limited edition copy at High5Journal.com. They incorporate everything that you've learned in this book into a simple daily journaling practice.

Turn the page and I'll show you the method and the science behind it. And there's a few blank journal templates to try. If you ever want more, you can download them for free at High5Journal.com.

How to high 5

1

Thanks to neuroscience, we know a stressed-out body puts your brain in survival mode and shows you threats instead of opportunities. So, all change requires you to settle your body first.

2

Take a deep breath. It's a powerful way to settle your nervous system, because it activates your vagus nerve. It's your secret weapon to creating instant calm in your body.

3

Hands on your heart is another way to tone your vagus nerve. This mantra is how you teach your body what it feels like to be safe and settled and access your calm and cool center.

4

Your senses are a conduit for the energy of your spirit. Begin to awaken that energy now to listen to it later.

5

Naming how your body feels is a key step toward deeper self-awareness and feeling comfortable with yourself.

6

My favorite daily habit to rewire the filter in your mind is to tell yourself that *you're worth cheering for, your dreams matter, and you can handle whatever comes your way.*

7

Once your body is calm, you can focus your mind and attention where you want it to go.

TODAY'S DATE: 12 5

⚡ Settle Your Body

Ground yourself in the present moment to get comfortable in your own skin.

☑ Take a deep breath

☑ Put your hands on your heart and say "I'm okay, I'm safe, I'm loved"

☑ What's one thing you can

See _I see bare trees out the window_   Hear _I hear my dog barking_

Touch _I feel my pen in my hand_   Smell _I smell freshly brewed coffee_

☑ In one word, I feel... _Busy_

☑ I deserve a High 5 today because _I got up on time this morning!_

☑ The next time you pass a mirror, prove it. Give yourself a High 5!

Clear Your Mind

To cultivate a confident mind, clear it of everything that's filling it right now: worries, tasks, doodles, thoughts, ideas, to-dos, or anything you don't want to forget.

Today is packed at work and I'm up against a big deadline. The dog needs to go out and is looking at me with these big eyes but I'll take her out as soon as I finish this. I need to call my mom back, she called and I feel guilty for not having called but I need to finish this deadline first. I woke up and immediately felt stressed by everything on my plate but I'm so glad I didn't look at my phone this morning and exercised to put myself first.

8

Clear your mind. Dump all your thoughts out onto the page. Don't hold back. Get it out of your head so that you can get into the present moment with yourself.

yourself every day

Free Your Spirit

A confident spirit is celebrating yourself and moving toward your desires.
Give yourself permission to get in touch with what you WANT.

WRITE 5 THINGS YOU WANT:

Big or small. Today or in your lifetime.

1. To free up my day to have more time for myself
2. To go on a trip every year to somewhere new
3. To get in the best shape of my life
4. To start a nonprofit related to improving mental health
5. To learn how to meditate and become more mindful

Describe the small actions you could take to inch closer to the things you want.

- More time for myself - I can schedule it into my calendar. I can set a time when I'll stop working and stick to it. I can make a plan to do a yoga class with a friend. I'll keep filling out my daily journal every morning. I am going to wake up earlier and use that time to work on writing a plan for the nonprofit.
-
-
-

NOW CLOSE YOUR EYES

Visualize taking these small actions.
Feel deeply what it feels like to do these things and move closer to what you desire.
This trains your body, mind, and spirit to help you take these actions.

9 Now your body is calm and your mind is clear. It's time to awaken your spirit.

10 Start dreaming in the morning! Write down five things that you want. Believe in them. Give yourself permission to have exactly what you desire.

11 Writing what you want will start to shift what you believe is possible as you rewire the filter in your mind. It also leads to a 42% higher chance of achieving your dreams!

12 Most people get manifesting wrong because they try to visualize the end result. Neuroscience research tells us to visualize yourself doing the hard, annoying, small steps along the way to reaching your dreams. In doing so, you tell your brain, "I do the hard work. I take advantage of opportunities. And I don't back down, I take action.

13 Brain scans have shown that you stimulate the same regions in your brain when you visualize yourself performing an action as when you actually do that same action, which makes you more likely to follow through on that action. And it's your actions that get results.

TODAY'S DATE: /

Settle Your Body

Ground yourself in the present moment to get comfortable in your own skin.

- Take a deep breath
- Put your hands on your heart and say "I'm okay, I'm safe, I'm loved"
- What's one thing you can

  See _____ Hear _____

  Touch _____ Smell _____

- In one word, I feel... _____
- I deserve a High 5 today because _____
- The next time you pass a mirror, prove it. Give yourself a High 5! 🙌

Clear Your Mind

To cultivate a confident mind, clear it of everything that's filling it right now: worries, tasks, doodles, thoughts, ideas, to-dos, or anything you don't want to forget.

Free Your Spirit

A confident spirit is celebrating yourself and moving toward your desires.
Give yourself permission to get in touch with what you WANT.

WRITE 5 THINGS YOU WANT:

Big or small. Today or in your lifetime.

1. _____

2. _____

3. _____

4. _____

5. _____

Describe the small actions you could take to inch closer to the things you want.

-
-
-
-
-
-
-

NOW CLOSE YOUR EYES

Visualize taking these small actions.
Feel deeply what it feels like to do these things and move closer to what you desire.
This trains your body, mind, and spirit to help you take these actions.

TODAY'S DATE: /

Settle Your Body

Ground yourself in the present moment to get comfortable in your own skin.

☐ Take a deep breath

☐ Put your hands on your heart and say "I'm okay, I'm safe, I'm loved"

☐ What's one thing you can

See _____   Hear _____

Touch _____   Smell _____

☐ In one word, I feel... _____

☐ I deserve a High 5 today because _____

☐ The next time you pass a mirror, prove it. Give yourself a High 5! 👐

Clear Your Mind

To cultivate a confident mind, clear it of everything that's filling it right now: worries, tasks, doodles, thoughts, ideas, to-dos, or anything you don't want to forget.

Free Your Spirit

A confident spirit is celebrating yourself and moving toward your desires.
Give yourself permission to get in touch with what you WANT.

WRITE 5 THINGS YOU WANT:

Big or small. Today or in your lifetime.

1. _____

2. _____

3. _____

4. _____

5. _____

Describe the small actions you could take to inch closer to the things you want.

-
-
-
-
-
-
-

NOW CLOSE YOUR EYES

Visualize taking these small actions.
Feel deeply what it feels like to do these things and move closer to what you desire.
This trains your body, mind, and spirit to help you take these actions.

TODAY'S DATE: /

Settle Your Body

Ground yourself in the present moment to get comfortable in your own skin.

☐ Take a deep breath

☐ Put your hands on your heart and say "I'm okay, I'm safe, I'm loved"

☐ What's one thing you can

See _____   Hear _____

Touch _____   Smell _____

☐ In one word, I feel... _____

☐ I deserve a High 5 today because _____

☐ The next time you pass a mirror, prove it. Give yourself a High 5!

Clear Your Mind

To cultivate a confident mind, clear it of everything that's filling it right now: worries, tasks, doodles, thoughts, ideas, to-dos, or anything you don't want to forget.

Free Your Spirit

A confident spirit is celebrating yourself and moving toward your desires.
Give yourself permission to get in touch with what you WANT.

WRITE 5 THINGS YOU WANT:

Big or small. Today or in your lifetime.

1. _____

2. _____

3. _____

4. _____

5. _____

Describe the small actions you could take to inch closer to the things you want.

-
-
-
-
-
-
-
-

NOW CLOSE YOUR EYES

Visualize taking these small actions.
Feel deeply what it feels like to do these things and move closer to what you desire.
This trains your body, mind, and spirit to help you take these actions.

Acknowledgments

First, I acknowledge myself. Yes, Mel Robbins, you deserve a huge round of applause. This book took 3 years, 2 publishers, 13 gigabytes of memory, 21 gallons of Phish Food ice cream, 7 boxes of tissues, and a few handfuls of Advil PM. This has been one of the hardest chapters of my life. Writing through it saved me and eventually this book appeared. I can't believe the shit I've been through (the lawyers won't let me say more) and still, here I am. I freaking did it. I am proud of myself. So, to me, Mel Robbins, I need to say: High F*cking Five.

To Melody, my extraordinary editor and wearer of killer red glasses: Do you even have eyelids? Because you never blinked once when I said, "I need another week/month/fiscal year." Who am I kidding? You'll probably edit that line out. I am so grateful I got to work with you. God, I love you.

To my entire team: With my hand on my heart, I thank you for not using my picture on a dartboard. Or maybe you did? Either way, I love you for sticking with me and this project, and for putting your heart into everything you do.

To the 55 people that have directly contributed to this book: I rewrote it so many times, I've forgotten many of your names. No seriously, I am grateful for your help. But especially to Tracey, Amy, Nancy, Nicole, Mindy, Stephanie, and Becca from Skye High Interactive. And I understand if you never want to see an email from me again.

To my literary agent, who I think has all but given up on me. Are you even reading this, Marc? You've broken the publishing mold. Thank you for your genius.

To Darrin, you were the first person that hired me for a paid speaking engagement because your wife, Lori, saw my TEDx Talk on Facebook. The rest is history. I tell everybody I would never be in this business without you two, and I mean it. And you tell everybody, "You have no clue what she's really like."

To Hay House: For allowing me to share all my insights and stories and not editing out the f-bombs. To everybody on the Hay House and Nardi Media teams—including Reid Tracy, Margarete Nielsen, Patty Gift, Betsy Beier, Michelle Pilley, Jo Burgess, Rosie Barry, Diane Hill, John Tintera, Karen Johnson, Tricia Breidenthal, Nick Welch, Bryn Best, Perry Crowe, Celeste Johnson, Lisa Reece, Lindsay McGinty, Ashley Bernardi, and Sheridan McCarthy—thank you. And thank you, Louise Hay. High five to you. And would you say hello to my grandparents in heaven if you see them—they're probably playing cribbage.

To Brendon Burchard and everyone that's a part of the High 5 Challenge: I love you.

To Jenny Moloney, who took amazing photos for this book (and Emily and Jess, the dream team that made me camera ready). Who knew how hard it was going to be to try to photograph a high five? Thank you for surviving that emergency landing, because the world needs more of your talent.

To my mom: The best and only mom I've ever had and ever will. You're a badass. The reason why I'm an entrepreneur is because of that stunt you pulled in Lumberman's Bank. I think the teller's jaw is still on the floor. Thank you for being my loudest cheerleader. I know I haven't made it easy at times.

To my dad: The kindest person I know. I can't wait for you to destroy me in a game of pool up in Vermont (in the brand new "pool table barn").

To Derek, you are my favorite brother, and his wife, Christine, *Hi*. No, seriously, thank you, BOTH of you, for having my back, saving my ass, and keeping me sane in more ways than I could publicly write.

To my father-in-law, Ken, thank you for delivering a message from heaven. Our son is the happiest he's ever been. And to my mother-in-law, Judie, who once so wisely observed "Mel, you always step in shit, but you always get out of it." It's not exactly poetic, but it's the truth, and I love you for always calling it as you see it.

To my best friends, Gretchen, Lisa, Bill, and Jonathan: We have ridden shotgun in each other's lives, and I so appreciate that we get to do life with you and your kids. I love you. You'll always be my best friends—because you know too much.

To Rose, the beauty from Brazil: Thank you for all you do. I love you.

To Yolo and Mr. Noodle, thank you for keeping me company when everyone else in the family went to bed.

To Sawyer, Kendall, Oakley: I know you think I'm a workaholic (and you're right), but to me it's not work when you love what you're doing. I dedicated this book to you and your dad because it's our greatest wish as your parents that you find the courage to pursue lives full of meaning, and that yours are as happy and fulfilled as you have made ours. From the bottom of my heart . . . thank you for cheering me on and supporting me as I have pursued my dreams. Also, I'm skipping family dinner tonight to take a Zoom call with my editor, Melody.

Chris, I love you the most. Thank you for loving me.

Bibliography

"Behavioral Activation Therapy Effectively Treats Depression, Study Finds." Harvard Health. Harvard Medical School Publishing, September 14, 2016. https://www.health.harvard.edu/mind-and-mood/behavioral-activation-therapy-effectively-treats-depression-study-finds.

"Female Reproductive System: Structure & Function." Cleveland Clinic. Cleveland Clinic's Ob/Gyn & Women's Health Institute, 2021. https://my.clevelandclinic.org/health/articles/9118-female-reproductive-system#:~:text=At%20birth%2C%20there%20are%20approximately,quality%20of%20the%20remaining%20eggs.

"Reticular Activating System." ScienceDirect. Elsevier B.V., 2021. https://www.sciencedirect.com/topics/neuroscience/reticular-activating-system.

"Understand Team Effectiveness." Google Re:Work. Google. Accessed April 29, 2021. https://rework.withgoogle.com/print/guides/5721312655835136/.

"Understanding the Stress Response." Harvard Health. Harvard Medical School, July 6, 2020. https://www.health.harvard.edu/staying-healthy/understanding-the-stress-response.

"Why Do We Take Mental Shortcuts?" The Decision Lab. The Decision Lab, January 27, 2021. https://thedecisionlab.com/biases/heuristics/.

Adolph, Karen E., Whitney G. Cole, Meghana Komati, Jessie S. Garciaguirre, Daryaneh Badaly, Jesse M. Lingeman, Gladys L. Chan, and Rachel B. Sotsky. "How Do You Learn to Walk? Thousands of Steps and Dozens of Falls per Day." *Psychological Science* 23, no. 11 (2012): 1387–94. https://doi.org/10.1177/0956797612446346.

Alberini, Cristina M. "Long-Term Memories: The Good, the Bad, and the Ugly." *Cerebrum* 2010, no. 21 (October 29, 2010). https://doi.org/https://www.ncbi.nlm.nih.gov/pmc/articles/PMC3574792/.

Alderson-Day, Ben, Susanne Weis, Simon McCarthy-Jones, Peter Moseley, David Smailes, and Charles Fernyhough. "The Brain's Conversation with Itself: Neural Substrates of Dialogic Inner Speech." *Social Cognitive and Affective Neuroscience* 11, no. 1 (2015): 110–20. https://doi.org/10.1093/scan/nsv094.

Amabile, Teresa, and Steven Kramer. *The Progress Principle: Using Small Wins to Ignite Joy, Engagement, and Creativity at Work.* Boston, MA: Harvard Business Review Press, 2011.

Baldwin, David V. "Primitive Mechanisms of Trauma Response: An Evolutionary Perspective on Trauma-Related Disorders." *Neuroscience & Biobehavioral Reviews* 37, no. 8 (2013): 1549–66. https://doi.org/10.1016/j.neubiorev.2013.06.004.

Beck, Melinda. "'Neurobics' and Other Brain Boosters." *The Wall Street Journal*. Dow Jones & Company, June 3, 2008. https://www.wsj.com/articles/SB121242675771838337.

Binazir, Dr. Ali. "Why You Are A Miracle." HuffPost. HuffPost, August 16, 2011. https://www.huffpost.com/entry/probability-being-born_b_877853.

Bohn, Roger, and James Short. "Measuring Consumer Information." *International Journal of Communication* 6 (2012): 980–1000.

Bolte, Annette, Thomas Goschke, and Julius Kuhl. "Emotion and Intuition." *Psychological Science* 14, no. 5 (2003): 416–21. https://doi.org/10.1111/1467-9280.01456.

Breit, Sigrid, Aleksandra Kupferberg, Gerhard Rogler, and Gregor Hasler. "Vagus Nerve as Modulator of the Brain–Gut Axis in Psychiatric and Inflammatory Disorders." *Frontiers in Psychiatry* 9 (2018). https://doi.org/10.3389/fpsyt.2018.00044.

Brown, Brené. *I Thought It Was Just Me (but It Isn't): Telling the Truth About Perfectionism, Inadequacy, and Power.* New York: Gotham Books, 2008.

Cascio, Christopher N., Matthew Brook O'Donnell, Francis J. Tinney, Matthew D. Lieberman, Shelley E. Taylor, Victor J. Strecher, and Emily B. Falk. "Self-Affirmation Activates Brain Systems Associated with Self-Related Processing and Reward and Is Reinforced by Future Orientation." *Social Cognitive and Affective Neuroscience* 11, no. 4 (2015): 621–29. https://doi.org/10.1093/scan/nsv136.

Cheval, Boris, Eda Tipura, Nicolas Burra, Jaromil Frossard, Julien Chanal, Dan Orsholits, Rémi Radel, and Matthieu P. Boisgontier. "Avoiding Sedentary Behaviors Requires More Cortical Resources than Avoiding Physical Activity: An EEG Study." *Neuropsychologia* 119 (2018): 68–80. https://doi.org/10.1016/j.neuropsychologia.2018.07.029.

Christakis, Nicholas A., and James H. Fowler. *Connected: The Surprising Power of Our Social Networks and How They Shape Our Lives.* New York, NY: Little, Brown, 2011.

Creswell, J. David, Janine M. Dutcher, William M. Klein, Peter R. Harris, and John M. Levine. "Self-Affirmation Improves Problem-Solving under Stress." *PLoS ONE* 8, no. 5 (2013). https://doi.org/10.1371/journal.pone.0062593.

Cross, Ainslea, and David Sheffield. "Mental Contrasting as a Behaviour Change Technique: a Systematic Review Protocol Paper of Effects, Mediators and Moderators on Health." *Systematic Reviews* 5, no. 1 (2016). https://doi.org/10.1186/s13643-016-0382-6.

David, Meredith, and Kelly Haws. "Saying 'No' to Cake or 'Yes' to Kale: Approach and Avoidance Strategies in Pursuit of Health Goals." *Psychology & Marketing*, 33, no. 8 (2016): 588–549. https://doi.org/10.1002/mar.20901.

Di Stefano, Giada, Bradley Staats, Gary Pisano, and Francesca Gino. "Learning By Thinking: How Reflection Improves Performance." Harvard Business School. Harvard Business School Working Knowledge, April 11, 2014. https://hbswk.hbs.edu/item/7498.html.

Duhigg, Charles. *The Power of Habit: Why We Do What We Do in Life and Business.* New York, NY: Random House, 2014.

Eagleman, David. *Livewired: The Inside Story of the Ever-Changing Brain.* New York: Pantheon Books, 2020.

Erdelez, Sandra. "Information Encountering: It's More Than Just Bumping into Information." *Bulletin of the American Society for Information Science and Technology* 25, no. 3 (2005): 26–29. https://doi.org/10.1002/bult.118.

Etxebarria, I., M. J. Ortiz, S. Conejero, and A. Pascual. "Intensity of habitual guilt in men and women: Differences in interpersonal sensitivity and the tendency towards anxious-aggressive guilt." *Spanish Journal of Psychology* 12, no. 2 (2009): 540-554.

Ferriss, Timothy. *Tools of Titans: The Tactics, Routines, and Habits of Billionaires, Icons, and World-Class Performers.* Boston: Houghton Mifflin Harcourt, 2017.

Firestone, Lisa. "How Do Adverse Childhood Events Impact Us?" *Psychology Today.* Sussex Publishers, November 12, 2019. https://www.psychologytoday.com/us/blog/compassion-matters/201911/how-do-adverse-childhood-events-impact-us.

Fitzpatrick, John L., Charlotte Willis, Alessandro Devigili, Amy Young, Michael Carroll, Helen R. Hunter, and Daniel R. Brison. "Chemical Signals from Eggs Facilitate Cryptic Female Choice in Humans." *Proceedings of the Royal Society B: Biological Sciences* 287, no. 1928 (2020): 20200805. https://doi.org/10.1098/rspb.2020.0805.

Fogg, B. J. *Tiny Habits: The Small Changes That Change Everything.* Boston: Mariner Books, Houghton Mifflin Harcourt, 2020.

Fredrickson, Barbara L., and Marcial F. Losada. "Positive Affect and the Complex Dynamics of Human Flourishing." *American Psychologist* 60, no. 7 (2005): 678–86. https://doi.org/10.1037/0003-066x.60.7.678.

Gabrieli, John, Rachel Foster, and Eric Falke. "A Novel Approach to Improving Reading Fluency." Carroll School. Carroll School, May 28, 2019. https://www.carrollschool.org/dyslexia-news-blog/blog-detail-page/~board/dyslexia-news/post/a-novel-approach-to-improving-reading-fluency.

Gabrieli, John. "Brain Imaging, Neurodiversity, and the Future of Dyslexia Education." Carroll School. Carroll School, October 1, 2019. https://www.carrollschool.org/dyslexia-news-blog/blog-dtail-page/~board/dyslexia-news/post/brain-imaging-neurodiversity-future-of-dyslexia-education.

Gallo, Amy, Shawn Achor, Michelle Gielan, and Monique Valcour. "How Your Morning Mood Affects Your Whole Workday." Harvard Business Review. Harvard Business School Publishing, October 5, 2016. https://hbr.org/2016/07/how-your-morning-mood-affects-your-whole-workday.

Howland, Robert H. "Vagus Nerve Stimulation." *Current Behavioral Neuro-science Reports* 1, no. 2 (2014): 64–73. https://doi.org/10.1007/s40473-014-0010-5.

Hyun, Jinshil, Martin J. Sliwinski, and Joshua M. Smyth. "Waking Up on the Wrong Side of the Bed: The Effects of Stress Anticipation on Working Memory in Daily Life." *The Journals of Gerontology: Series B*, 74, no. 1 (2019): 38–46. https://doi.org/ 10.1093/geronb/gby042.

Jarrett, Christian. "The Science of How We Talk to Ourselves in Our Heads." The British Psychological Society Research Society. The British Psychological Society, July 30, 2016. https://digest.bps.org.uk/2013/12/05/the-science-of-how-we-talk-to-ourselves-in-our-heads/.

Katz, Lawrence, Gary Small, Manning Rubin, and David Suter. *Keep Your Brain Alive: 83 Neurobic Exercises To Help Prevent Memory Loss And Increase Mental Fitness*. New York: Workman Publishing Company, 2014.

Kelly, Allison C., Kiruthiha Vimalakanthan, and Kathryn E. Miller. "Self-Compassion Moderates the Relationship between Body Mass Index and Both Eating Disorder Pathology and Body Image Flexibility." *Body Image* 11, no. 4 (2014): 446–53. https://doi.org/10.1016/j.bodyim.2014.07.005.

Kensinger, Elizabeth A. "Negative Emotion Enhances Memory Accuracy." *Current Directions in Psychological Science* 16, no. 4 (2007): 213–18. https://doi.org/10.1111/j.1467-8721.2007.00506.x.

Kluger, Jeffrey. "How Telling Stories Makes Us Human: It's a Key to Evolution." *Time*. Time, December 5, 2017. https://time.com/5043166/storytelling-evolution/.

Kraus, Michael W., Cassey Huang, and Dacher Keltner. "Tactile Communication, Cooperation, and Performance: An Ethological Study of the NBA." *Emotion* 10, no. 5 (2010): 745–49. https://doi.org/10.1037/a0019382.

Kross, Ethan, Emma Bruehlman-Senecal, Jiyoung Park, Aleah Burson, Adrienne Dougherty, Holly Shablack, Ryan Bremner, Jason Moser, and Ozlem Ayduk. "Self-Talk as a Regulatory Mechanism: How You Do It Matters." *Journal of Personality and Social Psychology* 106, no. 2 (2014): 304–24. https://doi.org/10.1037/a0035173.

LaMotte, Sandee. "The Other 'Fingerprints' You Don't Know About." CNN. Cable News Network, December 4, 2015. https://www.cnn.com/2015/12/04/health/unique-body-parts.

Lane, Andrew M., Peter Totterdell, Ian MacDonald, Tracey J. Devonport, Andrew P. Friesen, Christopher J. Beedie, Damian Stanley, and Alan Nevill. "Brief Online Training Enhances Competitive Performance: Findings of the BBC Lab UK Psychological Skills Intervention Study." *Frontiers in Psychology* 7 (2016). https://doi.org/10.3389/fpsyg.2016.00413.

Leary, Mark R., Eleanor B. Tate, Claire E. Adams, Ashley Batts Allen, and Jessica Hancock. "Self-Compassion and Reactions to Unpleasant Self-Relevant Events: The Implications of Treating Oneself Kindly." *Journal of Personality and Social Psychology* 92, no. 5 (2007): 887–904. https://doi.org/10.1037/0022-3514.92.5.887.

LePera, Nicole. *How to Do the Work: Recognize Your Patterns, Heal from Your Past, and Create Your Self*. New York, NY: Harper Wave, an imprint of HarperCollinsPublishers, 2021.

Levine, Peter A., and Gabor Mate. *In an Unspoken Voice: How the Body Releases Trauma and Restores Goodness*. Berkeley, CA: North Atlantic Books, 2010.

Madon, Stephanie, Max Guyll, Kyle C. Scherr, Jennifer Willard, Richard Spoth, and David L. Vogel. "The Role of the Self-Fulfilling Prophecy in Young Adolescents' Responsiveness to a Substance Use Prevention Program." *Journal of Applied Social Psychology* 43, no. 9 (2013): 1784–98. https://doi.org/10.1111/jasp.12126.

Masicampo, E. J., and Roy F. Baumeister. "Consider It Done! Plan Making Can Eliminate the Cognitive Effects of Unfulfilled Goals." *Journal of Personality and Social Psychology* 101, no. 4 (2011): 667–83. https://doi.org/10.1037/a0024192.

Masicampo, E.J., and Roy F. Baumeister. "Unfulfilled Goals Interfere with Tasks That Require Executive Functions." *Journal of Experimental Social Psychology* 47, no. 2 (2011): 300–311. https://doi.org/10.1016/j.jesp.2010.10.011.

Morris, Bradley J., and Shannon R. Zentall. "High Fives Motivate: the Effects of Gestural and Ambiguous Verbal Praise on Motivation." *Frontiers in Psychology* 5 (2014). https://doi.org/10.3389/fpsyg.2014.00928.

Moser, Jason S., Adrienne Dougherty, Whitney I. Mattson, Benjamin Katz, Tim P. Moran, Darwin Guevarra, Holly Shablack, et al. "Third-Person Self-Talk Facilitates Emotion Regulation without Engaging Cognitive Control: Converging Evidence from ERP and FMRI." *Scientific Reports* 7, no. 1 (2017). https://doi.org/10.1038/s41598-017-04047-3.

Mothes, Hendrik, Christian Leukel, Han-Gue Jo, Harald Seelig, Stefan Schmidt, and Reinhard Fuchs. "Expectations affect psychological and neurophysiological benefits even after a single bout of exercise." *Journal of Behavioral Medicine*, 40 (2017): 293–306. https://doi.org/10.1007/s10865-016-9781-3.

Nadler, Ruby T., Rahel Rabi, and John Paul Minda. "Better Mood and Better Performance: Learning Rule Described Categories Is Enhanced by Positive Mood." *Psychological Science*, 21, no. 12 (2010) 1770–1776 https://doi.org/10.1177/0956797610387441.

Oettingen, Gabriele, Doris Mayer, A. Timur Sevincer, Elizabeth J. Stephens, Hyeon-ju Pak, and Meike Hagenah. "Mental Contrasting and Goal Commitment: The Mediating Role of Energization." *Personality and Social Psychology Bulletin* 35, no. 5 (2009): 608–22. https://doi.org/10.1177/0146167208330856.

Oettingen, Gabriele, Hyeon-ju Pak, and Karoline Schnetter. "Self-Regulation of Goal-Setting: Turning Free Fantasies about the Future into Binding Goals." *Journal of Personality and Social Psychology* 80, no. 5 (2001): 736–53. https://doi.org/10.1037/0022-3514.80.5.736.

Pham, Lien B., and Shelley E. Taylor. "From Thought to Action: Effects of Process-Versus Outcome-Based Mental Simulations on Performance." *Personality and Social Psychology Bulletin* 25, no. 2 (1999): 250–60. https://doi.org/10.1177/0146167299025002010.

Ranganathan, Vinoth K., Vlodek Siemionow, Jing Z. Liu, Vinod Sahgal, and Guang H. Yue. "From Mental Power to Muscle Power—Gaining Strength by Using the Mind." *Neuropsychologia* 42, no. 7 (2004): 944–56. https://doi.org/10.1016/j.neuropsychologia.2003.11.018.

Richards, David A., David Ekers, Dean McMillan, Rod S. Taylor, Sarah Byford, Fiona C. Warren, Barbara Barrett, et al. "Cost and Outcome of Behavioural Activation versus Cognitive Behavioural Therapy for Depression (COBRA): a Randomised, Controlled, Non-Inferiority Trial." *The Lancet* 388, no. 10047 (2016): 871–80. https://doi.org/10.1016/s0140-6736(16)31140-0.

Robbins, Mel. *The 5 Second Rule: Transform Your Life, Work, and Confidence with Everyday Courage.* Brentwood: Savio Republic, 2017.

Roberts Gibson, Kerry, Kate O'Leary, and Joseph R. Weintraub. "The Little Things That Make Employees Feel Appreciated." Harvard Business Review. Harvard Business School Publishing, January 24, 2020. https://hbr.org/2020/01/the-little-things-that-make-employees-feel-appreciated.

Rogers, T. and K. L. Milkman. "Reminders Through Association." *Psychological Science*, 27, no. 7 (2016): 973–986. https://doi.org/10.1177/0956797616643071.

Rosenberg, Stanley. *Accessing the Healing Power of the Vagus Nerve: Self-Help Exercises for Anxiety, Depression, Trauma, and Autism.* Berkeley, CA: North Atlantic Books, 2016.

Rothbard, Nancy P., and Steffanie L. Wilk. "Waking Up on the Right or Wrong Side of the Bed: Start-of-Workday Mood, Work Events, Employee Affect, and Performance." *Academy of Management Journal* 54, no. 5 (2012). https://doi.org/10.5465/amj.2007.0056.

Runfola, Cristin D., Ann Von Holle, Sara E. Trace, Kimberly A. Brownley, Sara M. Hofmeier, Danielle A. Gagne, and Cynthia M. Bulik. "Body Dissatisfaction in Women Across the Lifespan: Results of the UNC-SELFand Gender and Body Image (GABI) Studies." *European Eating Disorders Review* 21, no. 1 (2012): 52–59. https://doi.org/10.1002/erv.2201.

Sbarra, David A., Hillary L. Smith, and Matthias R. Mehl. "When Leaving Your Ex, Love Yourself: Observational Ratings of Self-Compassion Predict the Course of Emotional Recovery Following Marital Separation." *Psychological Science* 23, no. 3 (2012): 261–69. https://doi.org/10.1177/0956797611429466.

Seligman, Martin. *Authentic Happiness: Using the New Positive Psychology to Realize Your Potential for Lasting Fulfillment.* New York: Atria Paperback, 2013.

Taylor, Sonya Renee. *The Body Is Not an Apology: The Power of Radical Self-Love.* Oakland, CA: Berrett-Koehler Publishers, Inc., 2021.

Texas A&M University. "Can You Unconsciously Forget an Experience?" ScienceDaily. ScienceDaily, December 9, 2016. https://www.sciencedaily.com/releases/2016/12/161209081154.htm.

The Power of Story, with Kendall Haven. YouTube. ABC-CLIO, 2010. https://youtu.be/zIwEWw-Mymg.

Torstveit, Linda, Stefan Sütterlin, and Ricardo Gregorio Lugo. "Empathy, Guilt Proneness, and Gender: Relative Contributions to Prosocial Behaviour." *Europe's Journal of Psychology* 12, no. 2 (2016): 260–70. https://doi.org/10.5964/ejop.v12i2.1097.

Traugott, John. "Achieving Your Goals: An Evidence-Based Approach." Michigan State University. Michigan State University, January 13, 2021. https://www.canr.msu.edu/news/achieving_your_goals_an_evidence_based_approach.

University of Hertfordshire. "Self-Acceptance Could Be the Key to a Happier Life, Yet It's the Happy Habit Many People Practice the Least." ScienceDaily. ScienceDaily, March 7, 2014. https://www.sciencedaily.com/releases/2014/03/140307111016.htm.

van del Kolk, Bessel. *The Body Keeps the Score: Brain, Mind, and Body in the Healing of Trauma.* New York, NY: Penguin Books, 2015.

van der Kolk, Bessel, Alexander C. McFarlane, and Lars Weisæth, eds. *Traumatic Stress: The Effects of Overwhelming Experience on Mind, Body, and Society.* New York: Guilford Press, 2007.

Wang, Yang, Benjamin F. Jones, and Dashun Wang. "Early-Career Setback and Future Career Impact." *Nature Communications* 10, no. 1 (2019). https://doi.org/10.1038/s41467-019-12189-3.

Willis, Judy, and Jay McTighe. *Upgrade Your Teaching: Understanding by Design Meets Neuroscience.* ASCD, 2019.

Willis, Judy. "Powerful Classroom Strategies From Neuroscience Research." *Learning and the Brain Workshop.* Lecture presented at the Learning and the Brain Workshop. Accessed April 29, 2021. http://www.learningandthebrain.com/documents/WillisHandout.pdf.

Willis, Judy. "The Neuroscience behind Stress and Learning." Nature Partner Journal Science of Learning. Nature Publishing Group, October 16, 2016. https://npjscilearncommunity.nature.com/posts/12735-the-neuroscience-behind-stress-and-learning.

Willis, Judy. "Want Children to 'Pay Attention'? Make Their Brains Curious!" *Psychology Today.* Sussex Publishers, May 9, 2010. https://www.psychologytoday.com/us/blog/radical-teaching/201005/want-children-pay-attention-make-their-brains-curious.

Willis, Judy. "What You Should Know About Your Brain." *Educational Leadership* 67, no. 4 (January 2010).

Willis, Judy. RadTeach. Dr. Judy Willis. Accessed April 29, 2021. https://www.radteach.com/.

Willis, Judy. *Research-Based Strategies to Ignite Student Learning: Insights from Neuroscience and the Classroom*. ASCD, 2020.

Wiseman, Richard. *The Luck Factor*. New York: Miramax Books, 2003.

Wolynn, Mark. *It Didn't Start with You: How Inherited Family Trauma Shapes Who We Are and How to End the Cycle*. New York: Penguin Books, 2017.

Wood, Dustin, Peter Harms, and Simine Vazire. "Perceiver Effects as Projective Tests: What Your Perceptions of Others Say about You." *Journal of Personality and Social Psychology* 99, no. 1 (2010): 174–90. https://doi.org/10.1037/a0019390.

About the Author

Mel Robbins is the leading female voice in personal development and transformation and an international best-selling author. Her work includes *The 5 Second Rule*, four #1 best-selling audiobooks, the #1 podcast on Audible, as well as signature online courses that have changed the lives of more than half a million students worldwide.

Her groundbreaking work on behavior change has been translated into 36 languages and is used by veterans' organizations, health-care professionals, and the world's leading brands to inspire people to be more confident, effective, and fulfilled.

As one of the most widely booked and followed public speakers in the world, Mel coaches more than 60 million people every month and videos featuring her work have more than a billion views online, including her TEDx Talk, which is one of the most popular of all time.

There's nothing Mel loves more than making a real difference in people's lives by teaching them to believe in themselves and inspiring them to take the actions that will change their lives. Mel lives in New England with her husband of 25 years and their three kids, but she is and will always be a midwesterner at heart.

WWW.MELROBBINS.COM

youtube.com/melrobbins

@melrobbins

facebook.com/melrobbins

@itsmelrobbins

@melrobbins

linkedin.com/in/melrobbins

We hope you enjoyed this Hay House book. If you'd like to receive our online catalog featuring additional information on Hay House books and products, or if you'd like to find out more about the Hay Foundation, please contact:

Hay House, Inc., P.O. Box 5100, Carlsbad, CA 92018-5100
(760) 431-7695 or (800) 654-5126
(760) 431-6948 (fax) or (800) 650-5115 (fax)
www.hayhouse.com® • www.hayfoundation.org

———

Published in Australia by: Hay House Australia Pty. Ltd.,
18/36 Ralph St., Alexandria NSW 2015
Phone: 612-9669-4299 • *Fax:* 612-9669-4144
www.hayhouse.com.au

Published in the United Kingdom by: Hay House UK, Ltd.,
The Sixth Floor, Watson House, 54 Baker Street, London W1U 7BU
Phone: +44 (0)20 3927 7290 • *Fax:* +44 (0)20 3927 7291
www.hayhouse.co.uk

Published in India by: Hay House Publishers India,
Muskaan Complex, Plot No. 3, B-2, Vasant Kunj, New Delhi 110 070
Phone: 91-11-4176-1620 • *Fax:* 91-11-4176-1630
www.hayhouse.co.in

———

Access New Knowledge.
Anytime. Anywhere.

Learn and evolve at your own pace
with the world's leading experts.

www.hayhouseU.com

NOTES

NOTES

NOTES

NOTES

📍 NORTH ATLANTIC OCEAN

4321

#HIGH5HABIT

Thanks for the 5 second rule ma'am @melrobbins 📖 I'm still using it on board ship and it's really effective. -Seafarer

mayazarya23

#high5habit @melrobbins

You Are SO AWESOMELY You!

DON'T LOOK IN THE MIRROR WITH GIVING YOURSELF A HIGH 5

natalia0.3

Don't forget to high 5 yourself every morning ✋

#HIGHFIVE @MELROBBINS

IGH5HABITS

Put the top down and blast the speakers

roxzesq

@MELROBBINS

HIGH FIVING MYSELF, BECAUSE @MELROBBINS !!

ljvcoaching

HIGH FIVE YOURSELF FOR YOUR EFFORTS!! BE YOUR OWN CHEERLEADER ~ INSPIRED BY @MELROBBINS 💀💀

4:33

logicmotivation

OH, BABY, YOU SHOULD GO AND LOVE YOURSELF

High five yourself, Love yourself. @melrobbins

YES!